WORKBOOK

# Focus on GRAMMAR 4A

FOURTH EDITION

# Focus on GRAMMAR 4A

FOURTH EDITION

Marjorie Fuchs
Margaret Bonner

with Jane Curtis

ALWAYS LEARNING

PEARSON

**FOCUS ON GRAMMAR 4A: An Integrated Skills Approach, Fourth Edition
Workbook**

Pearson Education, Inc., 10 Bank Street, White Plains, NY 10606

**Staff credits:** The people who made up the *Focus on Grammar 4, Fourth Edition,*
*Workbook* team, representing editorial, production, design, and manufacturing, are: Aerin Csigay,
Christine Edmonds, Nancy Flaggman, Ann France, Stacey Hunter, Lise Minovitz, and Robert Ruvo.

Cover image: Shutterstock.com
Text composition: ElectraGraphics, Inc.
Text font: New Aster

Photo credits: **Page 6** PictureQuest; **p. 18** WENN Photos/Newscom; **p. 22** Derek Storm/Splash News/Newscom;
**p. 27** Jumanah EI Heloueh/Reuters/Corbis; **p. 44** Jane Curtis; **p. 56** Shutterstock.com; **p. 62** UPI/Landov;
**p. 67** Shutterstock.com; **p. 74** Shutterstock.com

Illustrations: **ElectraGraphics, Inc.:** pp. 32, 50, 57

ISBN 10: 0-13-217008-6
ISBN 13: 978-0-13-217008-6

Printed in the United States of America

1 2 3 4 5 6 7 8 9 10—V001—16 15 14 13 12 11

# CONTENTS

# ABOUT THE AUTHORS

**Marjorie Fuchs** has taught ESL at New York City Technical College and LaGuardia Community College of the City University of New York and EFL at the Sprach Studio Lingua Nova in Munich, Germany. She has a master's degree in Applied English Linguistics and a Certificate in TESOL from the University of Wisconsin–Madison. She has authored and co-authored many widely used books and multimedia materials, notably *Crossroads, Top Twenty ESL Word Games: Beginning Vocabulary Development, Families: Ten Card Games for Language Learners, Focus on Grammar 4: An Integrated Skills Approach, Focus on Grammar 3 CD-ROM, Focus on Grammar 4 CD-ROM, Longman English Interactive 3 and 4, Grammar Express Basic, Grammar Express Basic CD-ROM, Grammar Express Intermediate, Future 1: English for Results,* and workbooks for *The Oxford Picture Dictionary High Beginning* and *Low Intermediate,* and *Focus on Grammar 3 and 4.*

**Margaret Bonner** has taught ESL at Hunter College and the Borough of Manhattan Community College of the City University of New York, at Taiwan National University in Taipei, and at Virginia Commonwealth University in Richmond. She holds a master's degree in Library Science from Columbia University, and she has done work toward a Ph.D. in English Literature at the Graduate Center of the City University of New York. She has authored and co-authored numerous ESL and EFL print and multimedia materials, including textbooks for the national school system of Oman, *Step into Writing: A Basic Writing Text, Focus on Grammar 4: An Integrated Skills Approach, Focus on Grammar 4 Workbook, Grammar Express Basic, Grammar Express Basic CD-ROM, Grammar Express Basic Workbook, Grammar Express Intermediate, Focus on Grammar 3 CD-ROM, Focus on Grammar 4 CD-ROM, Longman English Interactive 4,* and *The Oxford Picture Dictionary Low-Intermediate Workbook.*

**Jane Curtis** began teaching ESOL in Spain, where she participated in a Fulbright exchange program between the University of Barcelona and the University of Illinois at Urbana–Champaign. She currently teaches at Roosevelt University in Chicago, Illinois. She holds a master's degree in Spanish from the University of Illinois at Urbana–Champaign and a master's degree in Applied Linguistics from Northeastern Illinois University.

## UNIT 1 Simple Present and Present Progressive

### EXERCISE 1: Spelling: Simple Present and Present Progressive

*Write the correct forms of the verbs.*

| Base Form | Simple Present Third-Person Singular | Present Participle |
|---|---|---|
| 1. answer | answers | answering |
| 2. ask | asks | asking |
| 3. buy | buys | buying |
| 4. come | comes | coming |
| 5. do | does | doing |
| 6. eat | eats | eating |
| 7. employ | employs | employing |
| 8. fly | flies | flying |
| 9. forget | forgets | forgetting |
| 10. have | has | having |
| 11. hurry | hurries | hurrying |
| 12. lie | lies | lying |
| 13. open | opens | opening |
| 14. rain | rains | raining |
| 15. reach | reaches | reaching |
| 16. say | says | saying |
| 17. tie | ties | tying |
| 18. control | controls | controlling |

## EXERCISE 2: Simple Present and Present Progressive

Complete the conversations with the correct form of the verbs in parentheses—simple present or present progressive. Use contractions when possible.

A. **AMBER:** I _____think_____ I've seen you before. _____are_____ you
    1. (think)
_____taking_____ Professor Bertolucci's course this semester?
    2. (take)

    **NOËL:** No, but my twin sister, Dominique, _____is studying_____ Italian this year.
        3. (study)

    **AMBER:** That _____'s_____ her! I _____remember_____ her name now. You two
        4. (be)        5. (remember)
_____look_____ exactly alike.
    6. (look)

B. **JARED:** _____do_____ you _____know_____ that woman over there?
        1. (know)

    **TARO:** That's Mangena. She usually _____teaches_____ a pronunciation class at the Institute,
        2. (teach)

    but she _____is working_____ in the computer lab this term.
        3. (work)

    **JARED:** That's an interesting name. What _____does_____ it _____mean_____?
                4. (mean)

    **TARO:** I'm not sure. It's certainly not a name that's in style. I _____don't believe_____ I've ever
            5. (not believe)

    known anyone else with that name.

C. **ROSA:** How _____did_____ you _____spell_____ your name?
        1. (spell)

    **ZHUŌ:** Here, I'll write it down for you.

    **ROSA:** You _____have_____ unusual handwriting. It _____looks_____ very artistic.
        2. (have)        3. (look)

D. **IVY:** Hi. Why _____are_____ you _____sitting_____ there with such a terrible look
             1. (sit)

    on your face? You _____don't see_____ too happy.
        2. (not seem)

    **LEE:** I'm _____trying_____ to read this letter from my friend. He _____doesn't like_____ to
        3. (try)            4. (not like)

    use a computer, so he _____writes_____ his letters by hand and his handwriting
        5. (write)

    _____is_____ awful. It _____beginning_____ to get on my nerves.
    6. (be)        7. (begin)

E. **AMY:** _____do_____ you _____want_____ to hear something interesting? Justin
            1. (want)
_____is studying_____ to become a graphologist.
    2. (study)

    **CHRIS:** What exactly _____does_____ a graphologist _____do_____?
                    3. (do)

    **AMY:** A graphologist _____analizes_____ people's handwriting. You can learn a lot
        4. (analyze)

    about people from the way they _____write_____—especially from how they
        5. (write)

    _____sign_____ their name.
    6. (sign)

## EXERCISE 3: Simple Present and Present Progressive

*Complete the article. Use the correct form of the verbs in parentheses—simple present or present progressive. Sometimes there is more than one correct answer.*

Right now, Pam O'Neil _____is taking_____ a test, but she _____ it. She
                     **1. (take)**                                **2. (not know)**

_____ on what she _____, and not on how her handwriting
**3. (focus)**                      **4. (write)**

_____. The person who will analyze that test is a graphologist—someone who
**5. (look)**

_____ handwriting. Graphologists _____ that a person's
**6. (study)**                     **7. (believe)**

handwriting _____ an indication of his or her personality and character. These
           **8. (give)**

days, a number of businesses _____ graphologists. Handwriting sometimes
                      **9. (use)**

_____ employers to hire one job applicant over another.
**10. (convince)**

What exactly _____ company graphologist Perry Vance _____
                                            **11. (hope)**

to learn from applicants' writing samples? "I always _____ for clues to possible
                                      **12. (look)**

behavior," he explained. "For example, the slant of the writing actually _____ a
                                         **13. (tell)**

lot. _____ the writing _____ to the left or to the right? A left slant
                              **14. (lean)**

often _____ a shy personality. The position of the sample on the page is also
       **15. (indicate)**

important," Vance continued. "The right-hard margin of the page _____ the
                                      **16. (represent)**

future. Here's a writing sample from an executive who right now _____ a new
                                      **17. (plan)**

direction for a large company. Notice that this person _____ much room in the
                                **18. (not leave)**

right-hand margin. This is someone who _____ looking at the future."
                         **19. (not avoid)**

"What about signatures?" I asked. "Yes, signatures _____ us a lot about
                                  **20. (show)**

someone," said Vance, "Look at this one by a chief executive officer of a large firm. He

_____ on the news a lot these days because the federal government
**21. (be)**

_____ his company. Those very large strokes are typical of a person who
**22. (investigate)**

_____ about himself first and _____ advantage of other people."
**23. (think)**                                  **24. (take)**

Vance always _____, however, that his analysis _____ an
              **25. (warn)**                                **26. (not guarantee)**

applicant's future job performance. It's no substitute for careful review of a complete application.

## EXERCISE 4: Editing

*Read the email from a student to her favorite English teacher. There are ten mistakes in the use of the simple present and the present progressive. The first mistake is already corrected. Find and correct nine more.*

Dear Professor,

    Well, I'm here at my new school, and ~~I'm liking~~ *I like* it very much. I'm study in the English Institute this semester, and the style of the classes is really different from our English classes in Korea. My teachers doesn't know how to speak Korean, and my classmates are coming from countries all around the world, so we use English all the time. That is meaning that I'm getting a lot of good practice these days.

    Although I'm very happy, sometimes I'm having problems. I'm not understand my classmates' names because they don't look or sound like Korean names. I always ask the same questions: "What's your name?" and "How you spell it?" I want to use names with titles like "Mr. Hoffman" and "Prof. Li" for my teachers, but they want me to call them by their first names. It's difficult for me to treat my teachers so informally, but I trying. Slowly but surely, I'm getting accustomed to my life here.

    I miss you a lot. You still my favorite English teacher.

Hye Lee

## EXERCISE 5: Personal Writing

*On a separate piece of paper, write a paragraph about popular names in your home country. Use some of the phrases from the box.*

| | |
|---|---|
| In general . . . | These days . . . |
| In my country, people always . . . | We don't usually . . . |
| More and more . . . | We never . . . |
| Now, in the 21st century . . . | We sometimes . . . |

# UNIT 2  Simple Past and Past Progressive

## EXERCISE 1: Spelling: Regular and Irregular Simple Past Forms

*Write the correct forms of the verbs.*

| Base Form | Simple Past |
|---|---|
| 1. _____agree_____ | agreed |
| 2. _____ | applied |
| 3. be | _____ OR _____ |
| 4. become | _____ |
| 5. carry | _____ |
| 6. develop | _____ |
| 7. _____ | ate |
| 8. fall | _____ |
| 9. _____ | felt |
| 10. get | _____ |
| 11. grow | _____ |
| 12. live | _____ |
| 13. _____ | met |
| 14. _____ | paid |
| 15. permit | _____ |
| 16. plan | _____ |
| 17. _____ | sent |
| 18. sleep | _____ |

*Complete the magazine article. Use the correct form of the verbs in parentheses—simple past or past progressive. Sometimes there is more than one correct answer.*

# First Meetings
by Rebecca Hubbard

What _____were_____ you _____doing_____ when you first
**1. (do)**
_____ that special person in
**2. (meet)**
your life? A few months ago, we

_____ some couples to answer
**3. (ask)**
these questions. _____ it love at first sight, or _____ you
**4. (be)**
hardly _____ each other? _____ you _____
**5. (notice)**                                              **6. (go)**
out with someone else before you _____ your One True Love? Read some
**7. (find)**
of the great stories from our readers.

Dana and I sure _____ in love at first sight! We _____
**8. (not fall)**                                          **9. (work)**
in the same consumer research office when we _____. At the time the
**10. (meet)**
company _____ me, she _____ to get a promotion. It
**11. (hire)**                    **12. (try)**
_____ my very first job. I _____ a little scared, so I
**13. (be)**                              **14. (feel)**
_____ to know everything. Of course Dana _____ I
**15. (pretend)**                                          **16. (think)**
_____ to get the promotion instead of her. But then, one day I
**17. (want)**
_____ on a problem when she _____ into my office. I
**18. (work)**                              **19. (come)**
_____ her for help at first, but I was stuck, so finally I did. And guess
**20. (not ask)**
what! She _____ the problem! So then we _____ acting
**21. (solve)**                              **22. (stop)**
like opponents and treated each other like members of the same team. Eventually, we

_____ in love.
**23. (fall)**

**6**   UNIT 2

Van has been influential in my life since we were teenagers. We _____ 24. (take) the same high school social studies class when we _____. We 25. (meet)

_____ friends right away. At the time, I _____ someone 26. (become) 27. (date) else, and Van _____ interested in a romantic relationship. One day, the 28. (not seem) teacher _____ me while I _____ to Van. The teacher 29. (hear) 30. (whisper) _____ angry at us for talking during class, and she _____ 31. (get) 32. (tell) both of us to stay after school. I _____ to complain about such a severe 33. (want) punishment, but then I _____ my mind because I _____ 34. (change) 35. (realize) that staying late after school with a good friend might be fun. That afternoon, Van and I

_____ talking. We covered everything from our favorite music to our 36. (not stop) goals in life. As soon as I _____ with my old boyfriend, Van 37. (break up) _____ me out. 38. (ask)

Aleesha _____ into the apartment next door to mine when I 39. (move) _____ her for the first time. I _____ on the front steps 40. (see) 41. (sit) while she _____ to park a U-Haul moving truck in front of the apartment 42. (try) building. As soon as she _____ out of the truck, I _____, 43. (jump) 44. (think) "I'm going to marry that woman." I _____ her out right away because a 45. (not ask) guy _____ her move. He _____ like her boyfriend. 46. (help) 47. (seem) One day I _____ Aleesha and her "boyfriend" in the hall. She 48. (see) _____ me to her brother! I _____ her to dinner the 49. (introduce) 50. (invite) next weekend.

## EXERCISE 3: Simple Past and Past Progressive

*Use the cues to write sentences about Joao's first date with Dana. Use **when** or **while** and the simple past or past progressive form of each verb. There is more than one way to write some of the sentences.*

1. drops his wallet / waits for Dana in the restaurant

   *He dropped his wallet while he was waiting for Dana in the restaurant.*

2. drinks a glass of water / breaks the glass

   _____

3. stands up to greet Dana / falls on the wet floor

   _____

4. forgets Dana's name / wants to introduce her to a friend

   _____

5. eats a plate of spaghetti / gets some sauce on Dana's dress

   _____

6. has no money / gets the check at the end of dinner

   _____

7. thinks only about Dana / drives home

   _____

8. receives a phone call from Dana / recovers from his car accident

   _____

## EXERCISE 4: Editing

*Read the entry from Aleesha's journal. There are nine mistakes in the use of the simple past and the past progressive. The first mistake is already corrected. Find and correct eight more.*

December 16

                  **decided**

    I'm really glad that I ~~was deciding~~ to rent this apartment. I almost wasn't move here because the rent is a little high, but I'm happy to be here. All the other apartments I researched were seeming too small, and the neighborhoods just weren't as beautiful as this one. And moving wasn't as bad as I feared. My original plan was to take a week off from work, but when Hakim was offering to help, I didn't need so much time. What a great brother! We were moving everything into the apartment in two days. The man next door was really nice to us. On the second day, he even helped Hakim with some of the heavy furniture. His name is Jared. I don't even unpack the kitchen stuff last weekend because I was so tired. Last night I walking Mitzi for only two blocks. When I came back, Jared stood downstairs. I think I made him nervous because he was dropping his mail when he saw me. When he recovered, we talked for a few minutes. I'd like to ask him over for coffee this weekend (in order to thank him), but everything is still in boxes. Maybe in a couple of weeks . . .

## EXERCISE 5: Personal Writing

*On a separate piece of paper, write a paragraph about your favorite married couple (your parents, an aunt and uncle, family friends, etc.). Tell a story that shows why you really like them. Use some of the phrases from the box.*

| | |
|---|---|
| After they . . . | I felt . . . after . . . |
| As soon as . . . | I remember the time when . . . |
| Before this experience . . . | Let me give some background information . . . |
| Here's what happened . . . | They . . . while . . . |
| I chose to write about . . . because . . . | When I . . . |
| I didn't . . . until . . . | |

# Simple Past, Present Perfect, and Present Perfect Progressive

## EXERCISE 1: Spelling: Simple Past and Present Perfect

*Write the correct forms of the verbs.*

| Base Form | Simple Past | Past Participle |
|---|---|---|
| 1. become | *became* | *become* |
| 2. bring | | |
| 3. choose | | |
| 4. delay | | |
| 5. feel | | |
| 6. find | | |
| 7. finish | | |
| 8. get | | |
| 9. graduate | | |
| 10. hide | | |
| 11. notice | | |
| 12. omit | | |
| 13. own | | |
| 14. read | | |
| 15. reply | | |
| 16. rip | | |
| 17. show | | |
| 18. speak | | |

## EXERCISE 2: Contrast: Simple Past, Present Perfect, and Present Perfect Progressive

*A. Look at the reporter's notes about the bride and groom.*

### THE SKOAP–POHLIG WEDDING BACKGROUND INFORMATION

| Bride | Groom |
|---|---|
| Nakisha Skoap | Simon Pohlig |
| born in Broadfield | started doing extreme sports in 2004 |
| lived here all her life | moved to Broadfield in 2006 |
| B.A. Claremont College, 2005 | bought Broadview's historic Sharney's |
| 2002—Began working for | Restaurant in 2008; met Nakisha |
| Broadfield Examiner | Skoap at the restaurant |
| 2008—became crime news reporter | basketball coach for Boys and Girls Club |
| and started master's degree | 2007–2009 |
| program in political science | proposed marriage to Nakisha last year |
| started research on crime in | author of Simon Says and Duck Soup, |
| schools in Jan. | kids' cookbooks |
| Father—James Skoap, joined the | in Jan. started developing local TV show |
| Broadfield Police Department in | Mother—Tina Pohlig, fantastic chef. |
| 1989, retired in 2009 | Seven years as president of TLC |
| | Meals, Inc., but plans to retire soon |

*(continued on next page)*

**B.** *Write statements about the bride and groom, using the words in parentheses. Use the simple past, present perfect, or present perfect progressive form of the verbs. Add any necessary words to the time expressions.*

1. (Nakisha Skoap / live in Broadfield / all her life)

   *Nakisha Skoap has lived in Broadfield all her life.*

2. (she / graduate / from college / 2005)

   _____

3. (report / crime news / 2008)

   _____

4. (recently / research / crime in schools)

   _____

5. (work / on her master's degree / 2008)

   _____

6. (her father / work / for the Broadfield Police Department / 20 years)

   _____

7. (Simon Pohlig / move / to Broadfield / 2006)

   _____

8. (own / the historic Sharney's Restaurant / 2008)

   _____

9. (A friend / introduce / Simon and Nakisha / at the restaurant / one night)

   _____

10. (coach / basketball / for the Boys and Girls Club / two years)

    _____

11. (write / two cookbooks for children)

    _____

12. (plan / a local television show / January of this year)

    _____

13. (Nakisha and Simon / be engaged / one year)

    _____

**A.** *Look at Nakisha's job application. Then complete the personnel officer's notes on page 14.*

## CODEX MAGAZINE
## JOB APPLICATION

1. Position applied for: _____ Editor _____ Today's date: _Nov. 12, 2010_

2. Full legal name _Skoap-Pohlig_ _____ _Nakisha_ _____ _Ann_
         Last       First       Middle

3. Current address _22 East 10th Street_

   _Broadfield,_ _____ _Ohio_ _____ _43216_ _____ How long at this address? _5 months_
     City     State     Zip Code

4. Previous address _17 Willow Terrace_

   _Broadfield,_ _____ _Ohio_ _____ _43216_ _____ How long at this address? _1981–June 1, 2010_
     City     State     Zip Code

5. Education. Circle the number of years of post high school education.  1  2  3  4  5  6 ⑦ 8

6.

| Name of Institution | Degree | Major | Dates Attended |
|---|---|---|---|
| 1. Claremont College | B.A. | Journalism | 2001–2005 |
| 2. Ohio State University | – | Urban Studies | 2006 |
| 3. Ohio State University | | Political Science | 2008–present |

If you expect to complete an educational program soon, indicate the date and type of program.

_I expect to receive my M.S. in political science in January._

7. Current job. May we contact your present supervisor? _____ yes _x_ no

   Job Title _Reporter_ _____ Employer _Broadfield Examiner_

   Type of Business _newspaper_ _____ Address _1400 River Street, Broadfield, OH 43216_

   Dates (month/year) _9/2002_ to (month/year) _present_

8. In your own handwriting, describe your duties and what you find most satisfying in this job.

   _I am currently a crime reporter for a daily newspaper. I write local crime news._

   _I especially enjoy working with my supervisor._

*(continued on next page)*

**B.** *Complete the personnel officer's notes. Use the correct affirmative or negative form of the verbs in parentheses—simple past, present perfect, or present perfect progressive. Sometimes there is more than one correct answer.*

1. I ___have interviewed___ Nakisha Skoap-Pohlig for the editorial position.
   (interview)

2. She _____ for a job on November 12.
   (apply)

3. She _____ at the *Broadfield Examiner* for a long time.
   (work)

4. She _____ several excellent articles for that publication.
   (write)

5. She _____ that job while she _____ a college student.
   (find)                                    (be)

6. She _____ two schools of higher education.
   (attend)

7. She _____ classes at Claremont College in 2001 and _____ her
   (begin)                                                        (receive)
   B.A. there.

8. Then she _____ to Ohio State University.
   (go on)

9. She _____ classes in two different departments at Ohio State.
   (take)

10. She _____ a master's program in urban studies.
    (start)

11. She _____ a degree in urban studies, though.
    (get)

12. After a year, she _____ to study political science instead.
    (decide)

13. She _____ her master's degree yet.
    (receive)

14. She _____ on Willow Terrace most of her life.
    (live)

15. For the past five months, she _____ on East 10th Street.
    (live)

16. In our recent conversations, the company graphologist _____ asking the
    (recommend)
    applicant to come in for another interview.

17. He says that in question 8 of the application, Ms. Skoap-Pohlig _____ a space
    (leave)
    between some words when she mentioned her supervisor.

18. He feels that this means she probably _____ her supervisor yet about looking
    (tell)
    for a new job.

19. When Ms. Skoap-Pohlig answered question 8, she _____ her writing to either
    (slant)
    the left or the right.

20. The graphologist _____ to me yesterday that this indicates that she is a clear
    (explain)
    and independent thinker.

*Read the letter to an advice column. There are fourteen mistakes in the use of the simple past, present perfect, and present perfect progressive. The first mistake is already corrected. Find and correct thirteen more.*

Dear John,

           *been making*
  My grandson and his girlfriend have ~~made~~ wedding plans for the past few months. At

first I was delighted, but last week I have heard something that changed my feelings. It

seems that our future granddaughter-in-law has been deciding to keep her own last name

after the wedding. Her reasons: First, she doesn't want to "lose her identity." Her parents

have named her 31 years ago, and she was Donna Esposito since then. She sees no reason

to change now. Second, she is a member of the Rockland Symphony Orchestra and she

performed with them for eight years. As a result, she already became known professionally

by her maiden name.

  John, when I've gotten married, I didn't think of keeping my maiden name. I have felt so

proud when I became "Mrs. Smith." We named our son after my father, but our surname

showed that we three were a family.

  I've been reading two articles on this topic, and I can now understand her decision to

use her maiden name professionally. But I still can't understand why she wants to use

it socially.

  My husband and I have been trying many times to hide our hurt feelings, but it's been

getting harder. I want to tell her and my grandson what I think, but I don't want to ruin

his wedding celebration.

  My grandson didn't say anything so far, so we don't know how he feels. Have we been

making the right choice by keeping quiet?

      A Concerned Grandmother Who Hasn't Been Saying One Word Yet

## EXERCISE 5: Personal Writing

*Write an email to a friend about a new interest or hobby that you have. Use some of the phrases from the box.*

| | |
|---|---|
| At first, I didn't . . . | I've just . . . |
| Before I . . . | One of the best things about . . . |
| For the past several weeks, . . . | Since I . . . |
| I still haven't . . . | You won't believe it. I've been . . . |
| I'm amazed that I've already . . . | |

# Past Perfect and Past Perfect Progressive

## EXERCISE 1: Spelling: Regular and Irregular Past Participles

*Write the correct forms of the verbs.*

| Base Form | Present Participle | Past Participle |
|---|---|---|
| **1.** bet | *betting* | *bet* |
| **2.** _____ | breaking | _____ |
| **3.** cut | _____ | _____ |
| **4.** do | _____ | _____ |
| **5.** entertain | _____ | _____ |
| **6.** _____ | _____ | fought |
| **7.** forgive | _____ | _____ |
| **8.** _____ | leading | _____ |
| **9.** plan | _____ | _____ |
| **10.** practice | _____ | _____ |
| **11.** quit | _____ | _____ |
| **12.** _____ | _____ | sought |
| **13.** _____ | _____ | sunk |
| **14.** steal | _____ | _____ |
| **15.** sweep | _____ | _____ |
| **16.** swim | _____ | _____ |
| **17.** _____ | telling | _____ |
| **18.** _____ | _____ | withdrawn |

*Read the online article about Lang Lang. Complete the information with the affirmative or negative past perfect form of the verbs in parentheses.*

---

www.WikiWonders.com

Music superstar Lang Lang was born in Shenyang, China in 1982. By the time he was three years old, he ____had started____ taking piano lessons. According
1. (start)
to Lang, he _____ Liszt's "Hungarian
2. (hear)
Rhapsody No. 2" during a *Tom and Jerry* cartoon, and

he _____ to play classical music, just
3. (decide)
like the music in the cartoon. By the time he was five,

Lang _____ first place in a major
4. (win)
competition, and his family _____ the importance of giving their son the best music
5. (realize)
education possible.

   After Lang Lang _____ on his piano skills for several years, he finally received
6. (work)
admission to the Central Conservatory of Music in Beijing. As a teenager, he took first prize in a

number of international competitions because he _____ an opportunity to study
7. (have)
with some of the best teachers in China and because he _____ a great love of music
8. (develop)
and a strong desire to be the best. But Lang _____ all of his goals yet. Before his
9. (reach)
sixteenth birthday, he _____ to the U.S. to study at the Curtis Institute of Music in
10. (move)
Philadelphia. Not long after, he began his professional career. By the time he turned twenty, Lang

_____ one of the most popular and successful concert pianists in the world.
11. (become)
   In 2008, Lang Lang's popularity increased when he played at the Opening Ceremony of the

Beijing Olympic Games. Many people in the audience _____ to classical music
12. (listen)
before. They were surprised at the beauty and excitement of his performance and were suddenly

fans. Interestingly, Lang Lang _____ to participate in the ceremony not just to
13. (agree)
represent his home country or become more famous. He _____ a sports fan since he
14. (be)
was a boy, so he enthusiastically performed, gave interviews, and attended events throughout the

Beijing Games. He also signed a contract with his favorite athletic equipment company and soon

---

began wearing Adidas Lang Lang Gazelle sneakers on stage. Because he _____

**15. (bring)**

sports, fashion, and his superstar quality to the serious works of composers such as Mozart, Liszt,

and Stravinsky, *Time* added Lang Lang to its list of the 100 Most Influential People in the World in

2009. According to the magazine, along with other talented young musicians, Lang Lang

_____ the world of classical music.

**16. (transform)**

*For more on Lang Lang, visit* www.langlang.com.

## EXERCISE 3: Past Perfect: *Yes / No* Questions and Short Answers

*Look at the musician's busy schedule. Complete the questions about his day and give short answers. Use the past perfect.*

**1.** It was 6:00 A.M.

A: _____ *Had he gotten up yet?* _____

B: _____ *Yes, he had.* _____

**2.** The young musician was taking his morning jog.

A: _____ piano yet?

B: _____

**3.** It was 11:00 A.M.

A: _____ with

reporters by then?

B: _____

**4.** It was noon.

A: _____ his

parents yet?

B: _____

**5.** It was shortly before 6:00 P.M.

A: _____ his warm-up exercises?

B: _____

| Today | |
|---|---|
| **A.M.** | |
| 5:00 | get up |
| 6:00 | take a jog in the park |
| 8:00 | practice piano |
| 10:00 | meet with news reporters |
| 10:30 | play Ping-Pong to relax |
| **P.M.** | |
| 12:00 | have lunch |
| 3:00 | call parents |
| 6:00 | do warm-up exercises for concert |
| 7:00 | start performance |
| 10:30 | check the following day's schedule |
| 11:00 | go to bed |

*(continued on next page)*

**6.** It was 7:30 P.M.

A: _____ that evening's performance?

B: _____

**7.** At 11:00 P.M., he went to bed.

A: _____ the following day's schedule?

B: _____

## EXERCISE 4: Past Perfect Progressive: Affirmative and Negative Statements

*Read the situations. Draw conclusions, using the affirmative or negative past perfect progressive form of the correct verbs from the box.*

| cry | drink | laugh | pay | wash |
|-----|-------|-------|-----|------|
| do | eat | listen | rain | ~~watch~~ |

**1.** Mara wasn't in the living room, but her DVD player was on.

She _____ *had been watching* _____ *Tom and Jerry* cartoons.

**2.** The lights were off, and none of her schoolbooks were around.

She _____ homework.

**3.** The window was open, and the floor was a little wet.

It _____ .

**4.** There was half a sandwich on the coffee table.

Mara _____ the sandwich.

**5.** There was an unopened bottle of soda next to the sandwich.

She _____ the soda.

**6.** Mara came into the living room. There were tears on her face.

At first I thought she _____ .

**7.** I was wrong. Mara wasn't upset.

She _____ really hard because of what was happening in

one of the cartoons.

**8.** There was a stack of clean plates next to the kitchen sink.

She _____ dishes.

**9.** Mara could hear the TV from the kitchen.

She _____ to the cartoons from the kitchen.

**10.** I was surprised when I realized how late it was.

I _____ attention to the time.

## EXERCISE 5: Past Perfect Progressive: Questions

*A student reporter from a university newspaper is researching some background information before his interview with a famous musician. Use **when** and the words in parentheses to write his research questions. Use the past perfect progressive.*

**1.** He recorded his first successful CD. (he / dream of stardom for a long time)

*Had he been dreaming of stardom for a long time when he recorded his first successful CD?*

**2.** He finally received a recording contract. (How long / he / live in New York)

_____

**3.** He got his first job as a musician. (he / really work as a cook in a fast-food restaurant)

_____

**4.** He decided to enroll at the Berklee School of Music. (Where / he / study)

_____

**5.** He began his music classes. (Why / he / take courses in accounting)

_____

**6.** He realized he wanted to be a professional musician. (How long / he / play piano)

_____

**7.** He established his new scholarship program. (he / look for ways to help young musicians for a long time)

_____

*Complete the article. Use the past perfect or past perfect progressive form of the verbs in parentheses. Use the progressive form when possible.*

# A Pop Music Sensation

In 2009, American R&B singer Beyoncé Knowles had a worldwide hit with her "Single Ladies" video. But that was not her first success. The talented young star ___had been performing___ since
**1. (perform)**

she was a girl. Before they were teens, she and several of her friends _____ to
**2. (begin)**

sing professionally. By that time, she _____ music and dance for several years.
**3. (study)**

Beyoncé got interested in singing after she

_____ first prize in a talent contest in her
**4. (receive)**

school for her version of John Lennon's song, "Imagine." Before the

contest, her dance instructor _____ Beyoncé's
**5. (hear)**

incredible voice, and she _____ her student to
**6. (push)**

develop all of her skills. In 1997, Beyoncé _____
**7. (be)**

a singer-dancer for a decade when she signed a contract with

Columbia Records and became successful as a member of Destiny's

Child. She was just sixteen years old. By the time the group made its final appearance together

in 2006, Beyoncé _____ as a solo artist for some time. Since 2001, she
**8. (work)**

_____ in Hollywood movies, and of course she _____
**9. (star)**                                                    **10. (record)**

music. She _____ a top-selling album, and in 2004 her fans got what they
**11. (have)**

_____ for when she won five Grammy Awards in a single night. Beyoncé's
**12. (wait)**

popularity continued to grow with more albums, more movies, and more awards—both before

and after "Single Ladies."

## EXERCISE 7: Simple Past and Past Perfect in Time Clauses

*Look at some important events in Beyoncé Knowles's life and career. Determine the correct order of the phrases. Then combine the phrases and use the past perfect or past perfect progressive to express the event that happened first. Use the progressive form when possible. Use the simple past for the event that happened second. Add commas when necessary.*

**The Life and Times of Beyoncé Knowles**

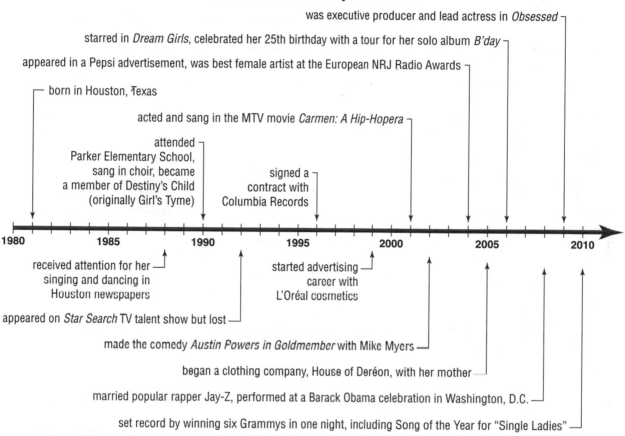

1. attended Parker Elementary School / received attention in Houston newspapers

    Before _Beyoncé attended Parker Elementary School, she had received attention in_

    _Houston newspapers._

2. lost the *Star Search* competition / signed a contract with Columbia records

    After _____

    _____

3. work at Columbia Records for several years / was in an ad for L'Oréal cosmetics

    _____

    by the time _____

*(continued on next page)*

Past Perfect and Past Perfect Progressive  **23**

**4.** filmed an MTV movie / made the comedy *Austin Powers in Goldmember*

Beyoncé _____

after _____

**5.** sang in a Pepsi ad / did ads for L'Oréal

When _____

already _____

**6.** start a clothing company with her mother / celebrated her 25th birthday

By the time _____

_____

**7.** acted for five years / starred in *Dream Girls*

_____

when _____

**8.** got married to Jay-Z / become internationally famous

_____

before _____

**9.** finish the movie *Obsessed* / performed at a Barack Obama presidential celebration

When _____

already _____

**10.** set a record by winning six Grammy awards in one night / earned millions from recording,

movie, and advertising contracts

By the time _____

already _____

*Read the review of a concert a student wrote for her school newspaper. There are ten mistakes in the use of the past perfect and past perfect progressive. The first mistake is already corrected. Find and correct nine more.*

My assignment for tonight was to see Lang Lang at Symphony Center. To be honest, I hadn't
expected much before I ~~had gone~~ *went* to the concert. In fact, I hadn't been look forward to it at all.
But then Lang Lang got my attention with his first two pieces.

By intermission, I had totally change my mind. Lang Lang had played just "Hungarian
Rhapsody No. 2," and the audience had gone wild. I had been hearing Lizst's composition many
times before, but not like that. By the time he finishes playing, everyone in the audience had
jumped to their feet and had started clapping enthusiastically. And the best part of the concert
had started yet.

After intermission, Lang Lang invited several young musicians to join him on the stage. All of
them had been winning a scholarship from the Lang Lang International Music Foundation. When
each child performed, I had felt their excitement and their passion for music. It was wonderful to
see that talented children could have a chance to succeed, regardless of their ethnic
background or financial situation.

Superstar quality was certainly on display tonight. As I left Symphony Center, I had to ask
myself a question. Lang Lang was absolutely incredible. Why I had taken so long to find out
about him?

*On a separate piece of paper, write a paragraph about an experience that surprised you.
Tell what you did. Then explain how the experience changed the way you thought and felt.
Use some of the phrases from the box.*

| | |
|---|---|
| Afterwards, . . . | I had an interesting experience . . . |
| As soon as . . . | I had never . . . before . . . |
| By the time it ended . . . | It happened . . . |
| I changed my opinion because . . . | When it started . . . |
| I had always . . . but . . . | |

# UNIT 5  Future and Future Progressive

## EXERCISE 1: Contrast of Future Forms

*Circle the best words to complete the conversation between two friends.*

1. **A:** Hi, Toni. Are you busy?

   **B:** Yes, I'm packing. Victor and I have plans. We'll go / (We're going) out of town tomorrow.

2. **A:** Do you need a bigger suitcase?

   **B:** Actually, I do.

   **A:** OK. I'm going to bring / I'll bring one over right away.

3. **A:** Do you take / Are you taking your dog on the trip?

   **B:** No. We can't. It's a business trip.

4. **A:** Your poor dog! He's going to miss / He's missing you.

   **B:** I know, but we won't be / we aren't out of town long.

5. **A:** So, give me some details about the trip.

   **B:** We're attending / We'll attend a World Future Society conference.

   **A:** When does the conference start / will the conference start?

   **B:** At 8:30 on Tuesday morning.

6. **A:** The phone is ringing.

   **B:** It's probably Victor. I'll answer / I'm going to answer it.

7. **A:** Watch out! The phone is on the edge of the table. It'll fall / It's going to fall.

   **B:** Relax. I have everything under control.

8. **A:** What are your plans for the conference?

   **B:** We'll see / We're going to see several presentations on Masdar City in the United Arab

   Emirates. Victor really wants to get a new job there, but he keeps promising me that

   he won't apply / he isn't going to apply for the job until we get more information.

9. **A:** I have to finish packing. Our plane will leave / Our plane leaves at 6:30 A.M.

 **B:** What? You've already completely filled my largest suitcase, and just look at the zipper.

 It'll break / It's going to break.

## EXERCISE 2: Future Progressive: Affirmative and Negative Statements

*Complete the article. Use the affirmative or negative future progressive form of the words in parentheses.*

# A Green City in the Desert

If all goes according to plan, as many as 50,000 people

_____ *will be living* _____ in super green[1] Masdar City in
    **1. (will / live)**
the United Arab Emirates in 2020. Amazingly, residents

_____ the comforts of modern life, but
    **2. (will / enjoy)**
they _____ the environment.
    **3. (will / harm)**

Although Masdar City will be located in one of the richest oil countries in the world, its

citizens _____ fossil fuel. They _____
    **4. (be going to / use)**                **5. (be going to / take advantage of)**
the sun and the wind as sources of power in their zero-carbon, zero-waste community.

 Construction is already underway on Masdar City. In the coming years, architects and

engineers _____ on creative ways to make this green city a reality.
    **6. (will / work)**
At the same time, graduate students at the Masdar Institute of Science and Technology

_____ research to develop innovative products and construction
    **7. (be going to / do)**
techniques to meet the challenges of this exciting project.

 One of the biggest challenges for any green community is transportation. The residents of

Masdar City _____. In fact, there will be no cars. People
    **8. (will / drive)**
_____ in small electric vehicles that will be part of the public
    **9. (be going to / travel)**
transportation system. Even better, they _____. After all, the
    **10. (will / walk)**
_____

[1]*green:* a. the color green (because of trees and plants) b. protective of the environment

*(continued on next page)*

streets of Masdar City will have protection from the sun and hot temperatures of the desert, and

with new technology, cool air _____ in from the nearby Persian Gulf.
                                       **11. (be going to / blow)**

  Speaking of water, residents of Masdar City _____ water from
                                                    **12. (will / drink)**

the Persian Gulf after the salt is removed from it in a solar powered plant. Then, additional

technology _____ the waste water so that it can be used for
              **13. (be going to / clean)**

farming and other purposes. And that's not all. When Masdar City is complete, it will be

totally waste-free. Workers _____ garbage to create power, and
                                  **14. (will / burn)**

they _____ materials for reuse and recycling.
        **15. (will / collect)**

  It will cost approximately $22 billion to build Masdar City, and the government of Abu

Dhabi _____ most of the bills. Officials there see it as smart
          **16. (will / pay)**

planning. If futurists are correct, more and more countries _____
                                                                 **17. (be going to / try)**

to follow the model of this eco-city in the desert sometime soon.


## EXERCISE 3: Future Progressive: Questions and Short Answers

*Complete the conversations. Use the future progressive form of the words in parentheses or
short answers where appropriate.*

**1. A:** When _will you be making your decision_____?
                          **(you / will / make your decision)**

   **B:** Tomorrow. It won't take long for us to decide who will be getting the job.

**2. A:** _____?
            **(the company / will / pay for my wife's airfare)**

   **B:** _____. Any job offer we give will include airline tickets for

   your entire family to Abu Dhabi.

**3. A:** Toni, _____?
                    **(you / be going to / travel alone)**

   **B:** _____. Victor and I are going to be on the same flight.

**4. A:** You're leaving so soon! Between now and the day you leave for Victor's new job, what

   _____?
                    **(you / be going to / do)**

   **B:** I have a lot of things to take care of, but we'll have time to go out for lunch. I promise.

**5. A:** Victor, _____?
(you / will / stop at the consulate office today)

   **B:** _____. The Masdar company assistant is taking care of all our

   travel documents. She's great.

**6. A:** _____?
(she / be going to / send the travel documents soon)

   **B:** _____. I expect everything to arrive in the next couple of days.

**7. A:** What kind of apartment _____?
(we / will / live in)

   **B:** Hey, stop worrying. Everything will be great in Masdar City. You'll love it.

**8. A:** How _____?
(we / will / get to the airport)

   **B:** I think that we should take a taxi.

## EXERCISE 4: Future Progressive or Simple Present

*Look at Toni's and Victor's schedules for tomorrow. Complete the statements. Use the correct form of the verbs—future progressive with **will** or simple present.*

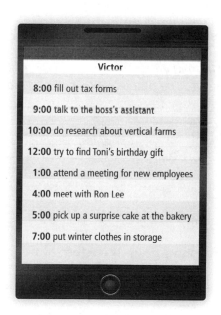

**Toni**

8:00 go to the post office
9:00 call the electric company
10:00 buy everything on the shopping list
12:00 eat lunch with Aidiya
1:00 visit Mom
4:00 take the dog to Brigitte's house
5:00 prepare dinner
7:00 finish packing

**Victor**

8:00 fill out tax forms
9:00 talk to the boss's assistant
10:00 do research about vertical farms
12:00 try to find Toni's birthday gift
1:00 attend a meeting for new employees
4:00 meet with Ron Lee
5:00 pick up a surprise cake at the bakery
7:00 put winter clothes in storage

1. While Toni _____*goes to*_____ the post office,

   Victor _____*will be filling out tax forms*_____ for his new job.

2. Victor _____ his boss's assistant

   while Toni _____.

*(continued on next page)*

3. Toni _____ on her shopping list before the trip to Masdar City,

   while Victor _____.

4. While Victor _____

   Toni _____ with Aidiya.

5. Victor _____

   while Toni _____ her mother.

6. While Victor _____ with Ron Lee,

   Toni _____.

7. Victor _____ at the bakery

   while Toni _____.

8. While Toni _____,

   Victor _____ in storage.

## EXERCISE 5: Editing

*Read Victor's journal entry. Victor has made ten mistakes in the use of the future and the
future progressive. The first mistake is already corrected. Find and correct nine more.*

>                *I'm going*
> It's 11:00 P.M. now. ~~I go~~ to bed in a few minutes, but I'm afraid that I won't
>
> get much sleep tonight. I'll be tired when I will get up, but I can't stop thinking
>
> about my new job. Toni has our last day here completely planned. In the morning,
>
> we're going have breakfast with friends and family. Then we're taking care of
>
> a few last-minute errands. Our plane will leave at 5:00 P.M., and Toni has
>
> already made a reservation for a taxi at 2:00. I'm really excited. At this time
>
> tomorrow, Toni and I will be sit on the airplane on our way to Abu Dhabi. If I
>
> know Toni, she is enjoying a movie while I will try to catch up on my sleep. Oh,
>
> no, I hear thunder. It will rain, so I'd better close all the windows. Maybe I'm
>
> going to watch the rain for a while. It's a long time before I see rain again.

## EXERCISE 6: Personal Writing

*Write a paragraph about a trip that you are planning. Use some of the phrases from the box.*

| | |
|---|---|
| Before I return home . . . | The best part of the trip will . . . |
| During the first part of the trip . . . | When I get back . . . |
| One day soon, I am going . . . | While I . . . , all my friends back home will be . . . |
| One thing is for sure. On this trip, I won't be . . . | While I'm there . . . |

# Future Perfect and Future Perfect Progressive

## EXERCISE 1: Affirmative and Negative Statements

*Complete the article. Use the affirmative or negative future perfect form of the words in parentheses.*

As of January next year, Pam and Jessica Weiner, two sisters

_____ **will have taught** _____ dozens of
**1. (teach)**

personal management seminars to grateful clients. Tired of

disorganization in their own homes, Pam and Jessica developed a

system that worked so well that they started teaching it to others. By

this anniversary celebration, hundreds of people across the country

_____ the Weiners' seminars, and these efficient
**2. (take)**

sisters _____ them manage the confusion and
**3. (help)**

stress in their lives.

"What a difference their seminars made!" exclaimed Terrie Smith, who completed the course

two years ago. "By the end of November, I _____
**4. (use)**

the system to complete my holiday shopping. I _____
**5. (purchase)**

all my gifts, and I _____ them too. I'll actually
**6. (wrap)**

have time to enjoy the holidays this year."

Why do we need a time-management system? According to Pam Weiner, statistics show that

people are extremely busy these days. For most of us, it seems that there are not enough hours

in the day, so we need to budget our time. Weiner gave an example of a new family in their

seminar. She said, "Ana and Jon are busy with their two children, and they both work.

However, they have no system, and this creates stress. By next Monday, the busy couple

_____ the week's menu yet, and they
**7. (plan)**

_____ on a driving schedule for the week's
**8. (decide)**

activities, which will cause a lot of problems. By the time Friday comes along, it is likely that

they _____ more than once about these things.
**9. (argue)**

As a result, they will feel frustrated, angry, and tired."

The Metcalfs, one of many satisfied families, agree. As Aida Metcalf explained, "At the end

of this week, we _____ a lot in a minimum
**10. (accomplish)**

amount of time, and we _____ our energy
**11. (waste)**

arguing about who does what in the house. Even better, because of our plan we

_____ all the housework by noon on Saturday
**12. (finish)**

and we can make plans to go out. Then, when we go back to work on Monday morning, we

_____ a good time for part of the weekend, and
**13. (have)**

we'll feel refreshed and ready to start a new week."

In the Metcalfs' experience, the time-management system also works well for long-range

planning. Aida said, "Before our seminar with the Weiners, our summers were a nightmare. We

never got to do the things we really wanted to do. But by the end of August this year, we

_____ in our community yardsale, and
**14. (participate)**

_____ the house. What's more, we
**15. (redecorate)**

_____ all the preparations for our annual
**16. (make)**

September family get-together."

Pam and Jessica Weiner will celebrate another anniversary when they are guests once again

on tomorrow's broadcast of *Around Town*. "Our television appearances started with this

show," Pam pointed out. "As of tomorrow, we _____
**17. (explain)**

our system to television audiences each Friday for an entire year."

## EXERCISE 2: Questions and Answers

*Look at the Metcalfs' calendar for August. Write questions and answers about their activities. Use the future perfect.*

### AUGUST

| SUNDAY | MONDAY | TUESDAY | WEDNESDAY | THURSDAY | FRIDAY | SATURDAY |
|---|---|---|---|---|---|---|
| **1** Aida walk 1/2 mi every day | **2** Arnie paint first bedroom | **3** Arnie paint second bedroom | **4** Arnie paint bathroom | **5** Aida start driving in carpool for day camp | **6** | **7** |
| **8** Aida water garden daily | **9** Corrie and Marsha pick vegetables daily | **10** | **11** Arnie paint downstairs | **12** | **13** | **14** Arnie put furniture back after painting |
| **15** | **16** Arnie 4:00 P.M. dentist appointment | **17** Arnie meet with banker to discuss ways to become debt-free | **18** Corrie pick blueberries for pies (need 3 quarts) | **19** Aida start baking pies for bake sale (agreed to bring 6 pies) | **20** Aida call Arnie's sister | **21** Community Center bake sale |
| **22** Aida start unpacking fall clothing | **23** Arnie plan menu for family get-together | **24** | **25** Iron and put away fall clothing | **26** Last day of summer camp for Corrie and Marsha | **27** | **28** Arnie go shopping |
| **29** Aida and Arnie pack for trip to Mom and Dad's | **30** Aida pay credit card bills | **31** Family travel to Aunt Irene's house | | | | |

1. (How many miles / Aida / walk / by August 31)

   **A:** *How many miles will Aida have walked by August 31?*

   **B:** *She'll have walked 15.5 miles.*

2. (Arnie / paint the bathroom / by August 5)

   **A:** *Will Arnie have painted the bathroom by August 5?*

   **B:** *Yes, he will.*

**3.** (How many rooms / Arnie / paint / by August 5)

A: _____

B: _____

**4.** (When / Arnie / finish all the painting)

A: _____

B: _____

**5.** (Aida / start driving the carpool / by August 6)

A: _____

B: _____

**6.** (on August 16 / Arnie / leave / for his dentist appointment / by 4:00)

A: _____

B: _____

**7.** (Aida / unpack / all the fall clothing / by August 23)

A: _____

B: _____

**8.** (How many quarts of blueberries / Corrie / pick / by August 19)

A: _____

B: _____

**9.** (How many pies / Aida / bake / by August 21)

A: _____

B: _____

**10.** (they / finish / packing for the trip / by August 31)

A: _____

B: _____

## EXERCISE 3: Future Perfect Progressive and Time Clauses

*Look at the Metcalfs' August calendar again. Complete the statements. Use the simple present and future perfect or future perfect progressive. Use the future perfect progressive when possible.*

1. By the time <u>Aida begins driving in the carpool</u>,
    **(begin driving in the carpool)**
    <u>Arnie will have been painting</u> for several days.
    **(paint)**

2. When _____,
    **(start the family get-together menu)**
    _____ for a couple of weeks.
    **(pick vegetables)**

3. _____
    **(call Arnie's sister)**
    before _____.
    **(do the menu)**

4. _____ already
    **(meet with the family's banker)**
    when _____.
    **(pay the monthly credit card bills)**

5. By the time _____,
    **(finish the fall clothes)**
    _____ for four days.
    **(work on them)**

6. When _____ on August 21,
    **(takes place)**
    _____ yet.
    **(finish summer camp)**

7. _____ for almost a week
    **(plan his special menu)**
    by the time _____.
    **(go shopping)**

8. By the time _____,
    **(travel to Aunt Irene's house)**
    _____.
    **(have a very productive month)**

## EXERCISE 4: Editing

Read the electronic ad. There are eight mistakes in the use of the future perfect and future perfect progressive. The first mistake is already corrected. Find and correct seven more.

# Find the Key to Your Future Success

*have*

By your next birthday, will you ~~made~~ your dreams come true, or will you have waste another 12 months of

your life? Will others have been enjoy fame and fortune for years when you finally decide to take action? Don't

wait any longer. The secret to your success is in our new book *Making Time for a Happy Future.* We guarantee

that you have found the formula for a better life by the time you will finish the last page of our incredible book.

Without a doubt, you'll have seeing the big difference that time management can make. Even better, you'll

have paid only $49.95 (plus tax and shipping and handling) when you receive the key to your future. Your

friends will not have received yet this offer. But you must act fast. Make your purchase now, or by this time

next week, you have missed the opportunity of a lifetime!

## EXERCISE 5: Personal Writing

Make a list of ten things you hope to accomplish by the end of the class(es) that you are
now taking. Put them in order of importance—from least important to most important. Use
some of the phrases from the box.

| | |
|---|---|
| By the time . . . | Most importantly, I will . . . |
| I will . . . before . . . | This class will end _____. By then, I . . . |
| I will have been . . . so I . . . | When the class is over, I will already . . . |
| If all goes according to plan, I will . . . | |

## UNIT 7 Negative *Yes / No* Questions and Tag Questions

---

### EXERCISE 1: Affirmative and Negative Tag Questions and Short Answers

*Anne-Marie wants to rent an apartment. Complete her conversation with the landlord. Use appropriate tags. Write short answers based on the apartment ad.*

> N. Smithfield unfurn. 1 BR in owner occup. bldg.,
> renovated kitchen w. all new appliances, incl.
> DW, near all transp. & shopping, $750/mo. + util.
> Avail. for immed. occup. Pets OK. 555-7738

1. ANNE-MARIE: *The rent is $750, isn't it?*

   LANDLORD: *Yes, it is.*

2. ANNE-MARIE: That includes electricity, _____

   LANDLORD: _____

3. ANNE-MARIE: The apartment isn't furnished, _____

   LANDLORD: _____

4. ANNE-MARIE: You've renovated the original kitchen, _____

   LANDLORD: _____

5. ANNE-MARIE: The kitchen doesn't have a dishwasher, _____

   LANDLORD: _____

6. ANNE-MARIE: You just put in a new refrigerator, _____

   LANDLORD: _____

7. ANNE-MARIE: A bus stops nearby, _____

   LANDLORD: _____

8. **Anne-Marie:** I can't move in right away, _____

   **Landlord:** _____

9. **Anne-Marie:** My pets won't bother you, _____

   **Landlord:** _____

10. **Anne-Marie:** You live right in the building, _____

    **Landlord:** _____

## EXERCISE 2: Negative *Yes / No* Questions and Short Answers

*Todd and a realtor are discussing two communities—North Smithfield and Greenwood.*
*Complete their conversation. Use negative* **yes / no** *questions to ask about Greenwood.*
*Write short answers based on the information in the box.*

> ## Greenwood—Community Profile
>
> Greenwood became a town in 1782. It has a number of historic buildings.
> **Schools:** Greenwood High School, Greenwood Community College
> **Shopping:** Greenwood Mall
> **Transportation:** local public bus
> **Recreational Facilities:** Briar State Park, Greenwood Beach (private),
> Davis Baseball Stadium (planned for next year)
> **Cultural Opportunities:** movie theaters (Greenwood Mall)
> **Average Rent:** $795

1. **Realtor:** North Smithfield has a community college.

   **Todd:** _Doesn't Greenwood have a community college?_

   **Realtor:** _Yes, it does._

2. **Realtor:** North Smithfield built a public beach.

   **Todd:** _____

   **Realtor:** _____

3. **Realtor:** There are historic structures in North Smithfield.

   **Todd:** _____

   **Realtor:** _____

*(continued on next page)*

4. **REALTOR:** You can see live theater performances in North Smithfield.

   **TODD:** _____

   **REALTOR:** _____

5. **REALTOR:** People in North Smithfield shop at a nearby mall.

   **TODD:** _____

   **REALTOR:** _____

6. **REALTOR:** The average rent in North Smithfield is under $800.

   **TODD:** _____

   **REALTOR:** _____

7. **REALTOR:** North Smithfield has been a town for more than a hundred years.

   **TODD:** _____

   **REALTOR:** _____

8. **REALTOR:** They're going to build a baseball stadium in North Smithfield.

   **TODD:** _____

   **REALTOR:** _____

## EXERCISE 3: Negative *Yes / No* Questions and Tag Questions

*Complete the conversations. Use the correct form of the verbs in parentheses. Write negative* **yes** / **no** *questions and tag questions.*

A. **ARI:** _____*Didn't*_____ you _____*move in*_____ last week?
                                    **1. (move in)**

   **DAN:** Yes. You haven't been living here very long yourself, _____*have you*_____?
                                                              **2.**

   **ARI:** Oh, it's been about a year now.

   **DAN:** It's a nice place to live, _____?
                                    **3.**

   **ARI:** We think so. We adjusted very quickly when we moved here.

B. **KATIE:** You haven't seen the letter carrier this morning, _____?
                                                         **1.**

   **DAN:** No. Why?

   **KATIE:** I don't think our mail is being forwarded from our old address.

   **DAN:** _____ you _____ one of those
                                        **2. (fill out)**
   change-of-address forms that the post office provides?

**KATIE:** Yes. But that was almost a month ago. We should be getting our mail by now,

_____?
                3.

**DAN:** I would think so.

**C.** **DAN:** _____ there an all-night supermarket nearby?
                    1. (be)

**MIA:** Yes. It's at 10th and Walnut.

**DAN:** I know where that is. _____ there _____
                                                                        2. (used to / be)

a restaurant there?

**MIA:** That's right. It closed last year.

**DAN:** That's strange. It hadn't been there very long, _____?
                                                                3.

**MIA:** About a year. I guess the location just didn't attract much business.

**D.** **ARI:** The new neighbors are really friendly, _____?
                                                                1.

**MIA:** Yes. That reminds me. The people across the hall invited us over for coffee and cake on

Saturday afternoon. You haven't made any plans for then, _____?
                                                                        2.

**ARI:** Well, I was going to work on our taxes.

**MIA:** _____ you _____ a little break?
                                            3. (can / take)

**ARI:** Sure. Why not?

---

## EXERCISE 4: Negative *Yes / No* Questions and Tag Questions

*The new tenants are going to visit their neighbors. They want to confirm some of the assumptions they have. Read their assumptions. Then write negative* **yes / no** *questions or tag questions. For some sentences, both types of questions are possible. (Remember: The only time you can use negative* **yes / no** *questions is when you think the answer is "Yes.")*

1. We think the people in Apartment 4F have lived here a long time.

   _The people in Apartment 4F have lived here a long time, haven't they?_ OR

   _Haven't the people in Apartment 4F lived here a long time?_

2. I don't think our apartment had been occupied for a while.

   _Our apartment hadn't been occupied for a while, had it?_

3. We believe this is a good building.

   _____

*(continued on next page)*

**4.** It seems that the owner takes good care of it.

_____

**5.** It looks like he has just finished renovations on the lobby.

_____

**6.** We don't think that he painted our apartment before we moved in.

_____

**7.** I have the impression he doesn't talk very much.

_____

**8.** I don't think the rent will increase next year.

_____

**9.** It looks like some new people will be moving into Apartment 1B.

_____

**10.** We have the impression that this is a really nice place to live.

_____

## EXERCISE 5: Editing

_Two students are preparing a role-play for English class. The lesson is about problems getting an apartment. There are ten mistakes with negative **yes** / **no** questions and tag questions in the dialogue. The first one is already corrected. Find and correct nine more._

**MARIAM:** You own this building, ~~didn't~~ _don't_ you?

**OWNER:** Yes. And you've been living next door for about a year now, have you?

**MARIAM:** That's right. But I'm interested in moving. There's a vacant apartment in your building, isn't it?

**OWNER:** Yes. It's a one-bedroom on the fourth floor. The rent is $900 a month, plus utilities.

**MARIAM:** Wow! That's a lot of money, isn't it? Could you not lower the rent a little?

**OWNER:** Wait a minute! You came over here to talk to me, haven't you? You want to live here, don't you?

**MARIAM:** No. I love this building. It would be perfect for me, but I can't pay $900 a month.

**OWNER:** But this is an historic structure. I was originally planning to charge $1,000 a month.

**MARIAM:** I know. The history is what attracted me in the first place. But the elevator isn't working, isn't it?

**OWNER:** No, it isn't. OK, so if I lower the rent, you'll do some things in the apartment like painting, won't they?

**MARIAM:** Definitely. And I'm going to pay $700 a month, amn't I?

**OWNER:** OK, OK. And you can move in next weekend, can you?

**MARIAM:** It's a deal!

## EXERCISE 6: Personal Writing

*Write questions about the place where you live, study, or work. Then find someone who will answer the questions for you. Use negative* **yes** / **no** *questions and tag questions to confirm information you think you already know. Use some of the phrases from the box.*

| . . . , are they? | . . . , don't they? | Isn't this . . . ? |
|---|---|---|
| . . . , aren't I? | Doesn't this building . . . ? | There are a lot of . . . ? |
| . . . , can it? | Haven't . . . ? | We won't . . . ? |

# Additions and Responses:
## *So, Too, Neither, Not either*, and *But*

## EXERCISE 1: Affirmative and Negative Additions

*Read the true story about twin sisters. Circle the correct words to complete the story.*

# Mirror, Mirror, on the Wall

Olga and Carmen Landa have gotten a lot of attention since they were infants. In fact, they remember being treated like rock stars in the small town in Venezuela where they grew up. It's no coincidence that people have always been interested in them because Olga and Carmen are mirror-image twins.

Mirror-image twins are identical, but they have opposite physical characteristics, personality traits, and preferences. For example, Olga writes with her left hand, but Carmen (doesn't)/ didn't.
                                                                                                                          **1.**
She's right-handed. Olga is outgoing and relaxed about life, but Carmen isn't / doesn't. She is
                                                                                          **2.**
very serious about making plans and getting things done as quickly as possible. According to the
sisters, Carmen has always been very organized and very neat, but Olga has / hasn't. Olga says
                                                                                          **3.**
that she doesn't mind if things are a little on the messy side. Olga has a strong fashion identity,
and so / too does Carmen. Olga doesn't like extreme styles. Neither / So does her sister, but
       **4.**                                                                      **5.**
that's where the similarities end. Olga is the sporty twin who prefers pants and comfortable
shoes, while Carmen wears skirts and high heels. Olga will buy clothes that are black or brightly
colored, but her sister will / won't. Her favorite colors are white or earth-tones like brown, beige,
                              **6.**
and yellow.

Being mirror-image twins doesn't take away from the strong connection that Olga and
Carmen feel. Olga can't imagine a life without her sister, and / but Carmen can't neither / either.
                                                                        **7.**                            **8.**
The two of them are best friends who have always been a pair. They studied together during
elementary school, high school, and university. After they worked for a few years, Carmen

decided to come to the U.S. to pursue her career in psychology. So <u>did Olga / Olga did</u>. It seems

**9.**

that when one of them gets an idea, the other one does <u>too / either</u>. If you ask them, the sisters

**10.**

will tell you they have always been the same, but always different.

## EXERCISE 2: Affirmative or Negative?

*Complete the conversations with affirmative and negative additions and responses.*

**A. KALEB:** I've heard that there's a twins festival every year.

    **KAREN:** _____*So have*_____ I.

                            **1.**

    **KALEB:** I didn't realize that there were enough twins around to have a festival.

    **KAREN:** I _____. But hundreds of them attended the festival last year.

                             **2.**

    **KALEB:** I'm talking about the festival in Twinsburg, Ohio.

    **KAREN:** I _____. Did you know that some of the people who go there actually fall

                       **3.**

          in love and get married?

    **KALEB:** Are you kidding?

    **KAREN:** No. In 1998, Diane Sanders and her twin sister Darlene went to the festival in Twinsburg,

          and Craig Sanders and his brother Mark _____. Diane and Craig fell in

                                    **4.**

          love, and _____ Darlene and Mark.

                         **5.**

    **KALEB:** Let me guess. Their children are twins.

    **KAREN:** Not exactly. Diane and Craig have identical twin sons, _____ Darlene and

          Mark _____. They have two singletons—one daughter was born in 2001

                       **6.**

          and the other in 2003.

    **KALEB:** What's a singleton?

    **KAREN:** A child that isn't a twin.

**B. ELLIE:** I thought I knew where the expression "Siamese twins" came from, _____

          I _____. I had to look it up.

                   **1.**

    **GRANT:** What did you find out?

*(continued on next page)*

ELLIE: Well, you know it refers to identical twins whose bodies are joined. Chang and Eng Bunker were conjoined twins who were born in Siam in 1811. The term was originally used to describe them. The preferred term today is "conjoined twins."

GRANT: I remember reading about them. Most doctors at the time had never seen conjoined twins, and _____ anyone else. Chang and Eng became famous.
2.

ELLIE: It's interesting. They ended up living in the United States. Chang got married, and _____ Eng. Their wives were sisters. Chang and his wife had 10 children,
3.
and Eng and his wife had 11.

GRANT: Do you know how they died?

ELLIE: When they were older, Chang was sick, _____ Eng _____.
4.
He was still strong and healthy. One night, Eng woke up, and his brother was dead. Eng died the same night.

C.    KIM: More and more women in the United States are having children later in life.

AMY: Women in Europe _____. The average age of new mothers is rising there.
1.

KIM: Because of the fact that new mothers are older and because of fertility treatments, the number of triplets, quadruplets, and quintuplets will continue to increase.

AMY: And _____ the number of twins.
2.

## EXERCISE 3: Affirmative or Negative

*Look at the information about twins festivals. Then complete the sentences about the festivals. Use the information in parentheses to write appropriate additions and responses.*

| Twins Festivals | | | |
|---|---|---|---|
| LOCATION | **Twinsburg, Ohio, U.S.A** | **Pleucadeuc, France** | **Beijing, China** |
| YEAR STARTED | 1976 | 1994 | 2004 |
| TIME OF YEAR | first week of August | mid-August | first week of October |
| WHO ATTENDS | twins, triplets, quads, quints, and their families | twins, triplets, quads, quints, and their families | twins and the general public |
| TYPES OF EVENTS | talent show, parade, contests, food, fireworks, photos | music, parade, photographs, food | entertainment, social events |
| COST | $15, additional costs for triplets, quads, and quints | free | free |
| REGISTRATION | recommended | recommended | none required |

1. Twinsburg, Ohio, has a twins festival each year, _____*and so does Pleucadeuc* OR *and Pleucadeuc does too*_____.
   (Pleucadeuc)

2. Twinsburg was holding its festival in the 1980s, _____.
   (Pleucadeuc)

3. Pleucadeuc doesn't charge an entrance fee, _____.
   (Beijing)

4. The Twinsburg festival isn't free, _____.
   (the Pleucadeuc and Beijing festivals)

5. Twinsburg will celebrate its festival next year, _____.
   (Pleucadeuc)

6. Twinsburg festival participants should register, _____.
   (participants at Pleucadeuc)

7. The Pleucadeuc festival doesn't have a talent show, _____.
   (the Beijing festival)

8. Twinsburg schedules its festival for August, _____.
   (Pleucadeuc)

9. Twins pay $15 at the Twinsburg festival, _____.
   (triplets, quads, and quints)

10. Pleucadeuc didn't sponsor a festival in 1990, _____.
    (Beijing)

11. Twins have gone to the Twinsburg festival for many years, _____.
    (their families)

## EXERCISE 4: Editing

*Read the online travel review. There are eight mistakes with additions and responses. The first one is already corrected. Find and correct seven more.*

# On the Road Reviews

**Twins Days Festival** ★ ★ ★ ★ ★

Twinsburg, OH

Twinsburg really knows how to throw a party! I went to the festival in 2010. My twin sister and
*did*
my cousins ~~do~~ too. We had a great time. I really enjoyed the line dancing, and so did my sister. I

had never done that kind of dancing before, but once I started, I couldn't stop, and neither can she.

To be honest, I was hoping to see a cute guy twin at the dance, and my sister did too, but we were

out of luck. I didn't meet anyone, and my sister didn't neither. But we still had fun. Our favorite

part was the picnic on Friday night. I loved seeing all the other twins there, and did my sister too.

I have always liked being a twin, but my sister has. The Twinsburg festival changed all that. By

Saturday morning, she was really excited. Of course I was too. We couldn't wait for the

Double-Take Parade to start. My sister and I both marched in the parade. I felt really proud and

excited to be a part of it. So she did.

Attending the Twins Day Festival with my sister may be a factor in why I liked it so much, but

my cousins aren't twins, and they can't wait to go back. My sister and I think the festival is

fantastic, and they are too.

## EXERCISE 5: Personal Writing

*On a separate piece of paper, write one or two paragraphs about yourself and the friend or family member that you resemble most. Use some of the phrases from the box.*

| | |
|---|---|
| Another similarity is . . . | The person that I resemble most is . . . |
| . . . does too. | We are really alike in . . . |
| . . . isn't either. | We have a lot in common. For example, . . . |
| Our greatest similarity is . . . | When I think about all that we have in common . . . |

# UNIT 9 Gerunds and Infinitives: Review and Expansion

## EXERCISE 1: Gerund or Infinitive?

*Complete the statements with the correct form—gerund or infinitive—of the verb **watch**. (Note: In some cases, both the infinitive and the gerund will be correct.)*

1. The children wanted _____ to watch _____ television.

2. I suggest _____ watching _____ television.

3. We would like _____ to watch _____ television.

4. Do you need _____ to watch _____ television?

5. I was busy, so I really couldn't afford _____ to watch _____ television.

6. I should have stopped, but I continued _____ watching _____ television.

7. Has a teacher ever encouraged you _____ to watch _____ television?

8. Some people dislike _____ watching _____ television.

9. Others absolutely refuse _____ to watch _____ television.

10. Please turn off all the lights after you finish _____ watching _____ television.

11. What time did you start _____ to watch _____ television?

12. My sister is addicted. She can't help _____ watching _____ television.

13. How long ago did you quit _____ watching _____ television?

14. Do you mind _____ watching _____ television?

15. My roommate and I have decided _____ to watch _____ television.

16. I feel like _____ watching _____ television.

17. They considered _____ watching _____ television.

18. He keeps _____ watching _____ television.

19. When you're tired, you seem _____ to watch _____ television.

20. Are they going to the movies or planning _____ to watch _____ television?

*Use the correct form—gerund or infinitive—of the verbs in parentheses to complete this article. (Note: In some cases, both the gerund and the infinitive will be correct.)*

# TOO ANGRY ___to remember___ THE COMMERCIALS?
**1. (remember)**

According to a new study, ___Watching___ violent TV
**2. (watch)**

shows makes it difficult ___to recall___ brand names or
**3. (recall)**

commercial messages. Violence creates anger, and instead of

___hearing___ the commercials, viewers are attempting
**4. (hear)**

___to calm___ themselves down after violent scenes. The
**5. (calm)**

conclusion: ___Sponsoring___ violent programs may not be appealing for advertisers
**6. (sponsor)**

because it may not be profitable for them.

This conclusion is good news for the parents, teachers, and lawmakers who have

objections to violence on television and are struggling ___to limits___ what children
**7. (limit)**

can watch. They had a small victory in the late 1990s, when lawmakers and the television

industry designed a TV-ratings system. Unfortunately, Congress did not ask parents

___to participate___ in ___createing___ the system, and the industry does not invite
**8. (participate)**     **9. (create)**

parents ___to preview___ shows before it assigns ratings. As a result, the system is not
**10. (preview)**

totally reliable, and parents are still guessing about the content of the shows their kids watch.

Why are parents objecting to ___haveing___ violence in television shows? The
**11. (have)**

numbers tell the story: A typical child will see 8,000 murders and 100,000 acts of violence

between the ages of 3 and 12! It's impossible ___to believe___ that this input won't
**12. (believe)**

affect young children. In fact, researchers have noted the following possible consequences

of ___viewing___ this much violence:
**13. (view)**

1. Children may become less sensitive to other people's suffering.

2. They may also become fearful of ___interacting___ with other people.
**14. (interact)**

3. They may be more likely ___to behave___ in a way that is harmful to others.
**15. (behave)**

Studies have shown that a majority of people want commercial TV _to produce_
16. (produce)
more educational and informational programs. In addition, more than 75 percent prefer

_to limit_ the number of hours of TV that children watch, and the American
17. (limit)
Academy of Pediatrics recommends _not permiting_ children _to watch_ more
18. (not permit)                                    19. (watch)
than one to two hours per day.

It's hard _understanding_ why the entertainment industry resists _makekeing_
20. (understand)                                              21. (make)
changes. Parents, teachers, and doctors are urging the industry _to develop_ clearer
22. (develop)
ratings and _to get rid of_ violence in children's shows. What's more, violent TV
23. (get rid of)
shows don't seem _to offer_ companies an effective way _to advertise_ their
24. (offer)                                              25. (advertise)
products. Even artists in the television business feel that it's time _to decrease_ the
26. (decrease)
amount of violence in American TV shows and have warned industry executives

_not to continue_ _to avoid_ change.
27. (not continue)  28. (avoid)
The industry may choose _not to pay_ attention to the public, but it will not be
29. (not pay)
able to ignore the government. Lawmakers want _to investigate_ the way networks
30. (investigate)
market violent shows to teenagers. They are also asking the industry _to schedule_
31. (schedule)
violence-free hours, when no violent content is allowed. Hopefully, parents in the United

States will someday feel good about _turning on_ the family TV.
32. (turn on)

## EXERCISE 3: Gerund or Infinitive?

*A TV talk-show host is talking to a doctor about children and TV violence. Complete the interview with the appropriate word or phrase from the boxes plus the gerund or infinitive form of the verb in parentheses.*

| fed up with | likely | ~~shocked~~ | unwilling | used to |
|---|---|---|---|---|

HOST: I was _shocked to learn_ that children will see 100,000 acts of violence on
1. (learn)
television before they are 12. I had no idea it was that bad. It also appears that the networks

are _unwilling to change_. They seem pretty satisfied with things the way they are.
2. (change)

*(continued on next page)*

Gerunds and Infinitives: Review and Expansion  **51**

**DOCTOR:** Yes, I think that they're ___used to putting___ all the responsibility on the viewer.
3. (put)

That's the way it's always been, and they're accustomed to it.

**HOST:** The networks may not want to change, but I know a lot of us are really very

___Fed up with seeing___ violence during family viewing times. We're really sick of it.
4. (see)

A lot of my friends don't even turn on the cartoons anymore.

**DOCTOR:** That's probably a good idea. Several studies show that children are much more

___likely to hit___ others after they watch violent cartoons. It's really
5. (hit)

quite predictable.

| decide | dislike | force | hesitate | stop |
|---|---|---|---|---|

**HOST:** OK. Now what can we do about this problem?

**DOCTOR:** Well, viewers can make a big difference. First of all, we have to put a lot of pressure on the

networks and ___force___ them ___to rate___ shows
6. (rate)

more clearly. They'll give in if enough viewers tell them they must.

**HOST:** What else?

**DOCTOR:** When you see something you don't like, pick up the phone immediately. Don't wait.

We shouldn't ___to tell___ the networks about material that we find
7. (tell)

offensive. Recently a network ___deciding to run___ a violent ad in some regions
8. (run)

of the country right in the middle of a family sitcom. So many people complained that they

reversed that decision and ___stop showing___ the ad in that time slot.
9. (show)

**HOST:** Violence bothers my kids, but they ___turning off___ a show once it starts.
10. (turn off)

They want to stick it out to the end.

| consider | forbid | insist on | permit |
|---|---|---|---|

**DOCTOR:** Parents have to assert their authority and ___insist on changeing___ the channel when
11. (change)

violence appears. Sometimes they'll face a lot of resistance, but they should be firm.

**HOST:** You know, in a lot of families, parents work until six. They can't successfully

___forbid___ their children ___from to turn on___ certain
12. (turn on)

shows. They're just not around to enforce the rules.

DOCTOR: There's help from the electronics industry in the form of a V-chip.

HOST: What exactly is a V-chip?

DOCTOR: It's a chip built into television sets. The V-chip doesn't __permit__

children __to tune in__ to violent shows. It blocks them electronically.
**13. (tune in)**

HOST: The V-chip and parental controls on satellite and cable TV are something all parents should

__Consider useing__.
**14. (use)**

| advise | agree | hesitate | keep |
|--------|-------|----------|------|

HOST: All right. Is there anything else that you __advise__ parents

__to do__?
**15. (do)**

DOCTOR: Parents must __keep communicateing__ with their children. They shouldn't
**16. (communicate)**

__keto ask__ their kids about their feelings and opinions—and especially
**17. (ask)**

about their activities.

HOST: Thank you, Doctor, for __agreeing to speak__ to us today.
**18. (speak)**

## EXERCISE 4: Objects with Gerunds and Infinitives

*Read the conversations about watching television. Then use the correct forms of the words in parentheses to write summaries.*

1.  KIDS: Can we watch TV now?

    MOM: I'm sorry, but you have to finish your homework first.

    SUMMARY: _____ *Their mother didn't allow them to watch TV.* _____
    **(their mother / allow / they / watch TV)**

2.  ANNIE: My parents finally bought me a new TV, but it has a V-chip.

    BEA: What's that?

    ANNIE: It's something that blocks violent shows so that I can't watch them.

    SUMMARY: __a V-chip interferes with Annie's watching violent shows.__
    **(a V-chip / interfere with / Annie / watch violent shows)**

3.  ROGER: Our kids really seem to like *Rappin' Reading*.

    CORA: I know. It's so great that there's high-quality TV about reading and learning.

    SUMMARY: __The show encourages them to get interesteing in books.__
    **(the show / encourage / they / get interested in books)**

*(continued on next page)*

4. **DAD:** You were having some pretty bad nightmares last night, Jennifer. I think you'd

better stop watching those cop shows.

**JENNIFER:** OK, but I really love them.

**SUMMARY:** her farther tells her not to watch cop shows anymore.
(her father / tell / Jennifer / watch cop shows / anymore)

5. **STUDENT:** We want to watch the TV news, but the reporting on adult news shows is usually

really frightening.

**TEACHER:** Try *Youth Views*. It's a great news program for kids.

**SUMMARY:** the teacher recommend them watching news for children.
(the teacher / recommend / they / watch news for children)

6. **SUE:** I'll never forget that great Knicks game we watched last year.

**BOB:** What Knicks game?

**SUE:** Don't you remember? We saw it together! The Knicks beat the Rockets 91–85.

**SUMMARY:** Bob didn't remember their seeing the game.
(Bob / remember / they / see that game)

7. **FRED:** Does Sharif still watch *Z-Men* every Saturday?

**ABU:** No. We explained that it was much too violent for him, and he decided not to

watch it anymore.

**SUMMARY:** Sharif's parent persuaded him not to watch the cartoon
(Sharif's parents / persuade / he / watch the cartoon)

8. **MOM:** Sara, it's nine o'clock. Time to turn off the TV.

**SARA:** Oh, Mom. Just a little longer, OK?

**MOM:** You know the rules. No TV after nine o'clock.

**SUMMARY:** the mother insisted on sara's turning off the TV.
(the mother / insist on / Sara / turn off the TV)

9. **AZIZA:** This is boring. What's on the other channels?

**BEN:** I don't know. Where's the remote control?

**SUMMARY:** Aziza wanted Ben to change the channel.
(Aziza / want / Ben / change the channel)

10. **PAUL:** *Primer Reportaje*, my favorite TV news program, starts in five minutes.

**NICK:** I've never understood why you watch that show. It's in Spanish, and you don't

speak Spanish at all.

**SUMMARY:** Nick can't get used to paul's watching a spanish languag
(Nick / can't get used to / Paul / watch a Spanish-language news program) news program.

*Read the student's essay. There are eleven mistakes in the use of the gerund and infinitive.*
*The first mistake is already corrected. Find and correct ten more.*

Asoka Jayawardena
English 220
May 30

# Violence on TV

    *hearing*
I'm tired of ~~hear~~ that violence on TV causes violence at home, in school, and on

the streets. Almost all young people watch TV, but not all of them are involved in

    *Committed*                  *to act*
committing crimes! In fact, very few people choose acting in violent ways. To watching

TV, therefore, is not the cause.

                                  *to make*
    Groups like the American Medical Society should stop making a point of to telling

          *to live*                                 *to have*
people what to watch. If we want living in a free society, it is necessary having

                   *to*  *need*
freedom of choice. Children need learn values from their parents. It should be the

          *to decide*
parents' responsibility alone deciding what their child can or cannot watch. The

                              *interfering*
government and other interest groups should avoid to interfere in these personal

   *to Limit*                                        *teaching*
decisions. Limiting our freedom of choice is not the answer. If parents teach their

    *to respect*               *enjoing*  *watching*
children respecting life, children can enjoy to watch TV without any negative effects.

---

*On a separate piece of paper, write a paragraph about a television show that you feel*
*everyone, both adults and children, should watch. Use some of the phrases from the box.*

| | |
|---|---|
| I can't remember . . . | The show will allow . . . |
| I really like . . . | These days, it is not easy . . . |
| I recommend . . . | This is a wonderful show for anyone who wants . . . |
| In addition to . . . | Watching this show is . . . |
| The program is a great way . . . | Without a doubt, everyone will enjoy . . . |

**EXERCISE 1: Contrast:** *Make, Have, Let, Help*, and *Get*

*Complete the article about the roles that animals can play in our lives. Circle the correct verbs.*

## The Animal–Human Connection

Can pets get / (help) humans lead better lives? Not only animal lovers but also some
1.

health-care professionals believe that pets let / get us improve our quality of everyday living.
2.

Pets have / help their owners stay healthy. For example, dogs need daily exercise, and
3.

this has / makes many owners turn off their television sets or computers and go outside for
4.

a walk. While walking their dogs, they get the health rewards of being physically active,

and they are able to talk to the people they see on the street or in the park. These positive

human relationships get / make dog owners feel happy, which can lead to longer, healthier
5.

lives. Speaking of positive relationships, it is interesting to note that research shows pet

owners often have lower blood pressure as a result of spending time with their animals. It

seems that pets get / make their owners to relax.
6.

Animals can also play an important role for humans who are sick. In some cases,

health-care professionals let / get animals to provide
7.

attention, affection, and companionship for their patients.

The animals don't replace other forms of medical care,

but they help / have patients recover more quickly and live
8.

longer. The Delta Society is a nonprofit organization that

promotes the idea of using animals in places such as hospitals, nursing homes, and

rehabilitation centers. The society lets / gets volunteers to work with those in need, but it
                                     9.

doesn't let / make just any pet participate in its programs. It makes / gets pets and their
         10.                                                      11.

owners complete training courses so that the animals will be friendly and give comfort to

the humans they meet.

   In addition to helping those who are ill, animals can assist people with disabilities.

Guide dogs help / make people who are blind cross busy streets or take public
              12.

transportation. People who are unable to move their arms or legs can help / have their dogs
                                                                        13.

open doors, turn lights off and on, and even answer the telephone. Special hearing dogs

make / let hearing-impaired owners pay attention when the doorbell rings, their baby cries,
   14.

or a fire alarm sounds.

## EXERCISE 2: *Make, Have, Get*, and *Help* + Object

*Read the tip sheet from an animal welfare agency. Complete the sentences by adding
pronoun objects and the correct form of the verbs in parentheses.*

# Dogs Are Family Members Too

Whether your family has a dog or you'd like to bring a dog

into your home, here are some things to consider.

### If you're thinking about getting a dog . . .

• It takes time and money to care for a dog. Be sure that you have enough of both. A dog could be a

   member of your family for 15 years or more.

• Talking to everyone in your family will make _____ *them feel* _____ part of the
                                                      1. (feel)

   decision-making process, and they'll be more likely to welcome a dog as a new member of the family.

• Pets are not always welcome. As one former pet owner says, find out if your landlord will let

   _____ you _____ a dog in your apartment.
         2. (keep)

*(continued on next page)*

- There are always animals available for adoption. Before buying a dog from a pet shop or a breeder, contact your local animal shelter. It's the humane thing to do. At the shelter, ask about classes or an adoption program that will help _____ what kind of dog is best for you and
  _you_ _to_ **3. (decide)**
  your family. Also talk to staff members about the health and history of a dog that you want to adopt. It's a good idea to have _____ you as much information as possible.
  _them_ **4. (give)**

### If there are children in the family . . .

- Your child may really want a dog, and she may promise to take care of your family's new pet, but honestly, it may be impossible to get _____ it. Consider dividing pet-care
  **5. (do)** _you to_ _decide_
  responsibilities among all members of the family, including children. It doesn't have to be complicated. Depending on the children's ages, it's certainly possible to have _____
  _them_ **6. (take care of)** _give_
  specific tasks such as taking the dog for a walk after school or giving the dog food and water.

- Children may have to learn to be gentle. Get _____ animals need respect
  **7. (realize)**
  just like humans, and that means no hitting, kicking, riding, or pulling the tail of the family dog.

- At some point, your dog will get overexcited when he is playing. Children should know what to do to get
  _____.
  **8. (calm down)**
- It pays to be careful. If you have a very young child, she may love the family pet, but never let
  _____ with the family dog alone. Adult supervision is essential.
  **9. (play)**

### If there is a new baby coming into the family . . .

- Your dog will know that there's been a change, and he will probably be excited, anxious, and quite curious. It's up to you to help _____. Before the baby arrives, introduce
  **10. (adjust)**
  him to baby sounds. He should also get accustomed to seeing a baby, so it's a good idea to use a doll or
  let _____ time around a real infant if possible.
  **11. (spend)**
- Your dog may need training so that you can get _____ you at all times
  **12. (obey)**
  when he is around the new baby. Remember to use positive rewards, not punishment.

- Although you'll be very busy with your new baby, spending some time with your dog will make
  _____ that he is still an important member of the family. It will also help
  **13. (understand)**
  _____ during this very exciting time in your life.
  **14. (relax)**

If you want to know more, contact our organization and let _____ you with
**15. (provide)**
more detailed information on dogs and families.

*Read the conversations. Then use the correct forms of the verbs in parentheses to complete the summaries. Add pronouns when necessary.*

1.  JOHN:   Mom, can I get a horse?

    MOTHER:  No, of course you can't get a horse!

    SUMMARY:  John's mother _____ *didn't let him get a horse.* _____
                                                        **(let)**

2.  MOTHER:  Instead of a horse, will you agree to adopt a dog or a cat?

    JOHN:   OK.

    SUMMARY:  John's mother _____
                                                        **(get)**

3.  MOTHER:  You can make the choice.

    JOHN:   I'd rather have a cat.

    SUMMARY:  His mother _____
                                                        **(let)**

4.  MOTHER:  Now, you have to do some research on pet care.

    JOHN:   I can do that. I know a couple of animal-protection groups that have good

            information on their websites.

    SUMMARY:  She _____
                                                        **(make)**

5.  JOHN:   Do I have to do all of the research by myself?

    MOTHER:  Yes, you do.

    SUMMARY:  John's mother _____
                                                        **(help)**

6.  JOHN:   I found out that I have to be 18 to adopt a pet. Can you fill out and sign the adoption

            application forms for me?

    MOTHER:  Sure.

    SUMMARY:  John _____
                                                        **(get)**

7.  MOTHER:  First, you have to explain the adoption process to me.

    JOHN:   I have all of the information right here.

    SUMMARY:  John's mother _____
                                                        **(have)**

8.  JOHN:   I have enough money to pay the adoption fees.

    MOTHER:  You may need the money later. I'll pay the fees.

    SUMMARY:  John's mother _____
                                                        **(make)**

## EXERCISE 4: Editing

*Read the university student's email. She made seven mistakes in the use of* **make, have,
let, help,** *and* **get***. The first mistake is already corrected. Find and correct six more.*

Hi, Ami!

Thanks for staying in touch. Your emails always make me ~~to smile~~ *smile*—even when I'm feeling

stressed. Knowing that I have a good friend like you really helps me relaxing and not take

things so seriously.

At the end of last semester, my roommates and I decided to get a dog. Actually, my

roommates made the decision and then got me go along with it. I made them promise to

take care of the dog, but guess who's doing most of the work?! Don't misunderstand me. I

love Ellie and appreciate what a great companion she is. I take her for a walk every morning

and every night and make her run and play in the park near our apartment as often as I can

because I know how much she enjoys it. Still, I wish I could have my roommates to spend

just an hour a week with "our" dog. At this point, I can't even get them feeding Ellie, and now

they want to move to an apartment complex that won't let us to have a dog. I think I'm going

to have to choose whether to live with my roommates or with Ellie—and I think I'm going to

choose Ellie!

Neha

## EXERCISE 5: Personal Writing

*On a separate piece of paper, write a paragraph about an experience with a pet. It can be
your own experience, or one you've learned about from a friend, a TV show, or a movie. Use
some of the phrases from the box.*

| | |
|---|---|
| I had to help . . . | Pets make me . . . |
| I was happy when I got the animal . . . | When it comes to pets, I would . . . |
| In my opinion, having a pet is . . . | You can always get . . . |

# UNIT 11    Phrasal Verbs: Review

## EXERCISE 1: Particles

*Complete the phrasal verbs with particles from the box. You will use some particles more than once.*

| ahead | down | on | over |
|-------|------|------|------|
| back | off | out | up |

**Phrasal Verb**                     **Meaning**

1. catch ____on____                  *become popular*

2. cheer _____                  *make someone feel happier*

3. do _____                     *do again*

4. get _____                    *make progress, succeed*

5. let _____                    *allow to leave*

6. let _____                    *disappoint*

7. look _____                   *examine*

8. pick _____                   *select or identify*

9. take _____                   *return*

10. try _____                   *use to find out if it works*

11. turn _____                  *raise the volume*

12. turn _____                  *lower the volume*

13. use _____                   *consume*

14. write _____                 *write on a piece of paper*

15. put _____                   *delay*

16. think _____                 *invent*

Read about New Year traditions around the world. Complete the article with the correct forms of the phrasal verbs from the box. Choose the verbs that are closest in meaning to the words in parentheses.

| burn up | get together | go back | ~~pay back~~ | put together | throw away |
|---|---|---|---|---|---|
| cut down | give out | go out | put on | set up | |

# Starting New

Wearing new clothes, _____paying back_____
                              **1. (repay)**

debts, lighting candles—many cultures share similar

New Year traditions. In Iran, for example, people

celebrate *Now Ruz*, or New Day, on the first day of

spring. A few days before the festival, families _____ bushes and
                                                    **2. (bring down by cutting)**

_____ piles of wood. They set the piles on fire, and before the wood
   **3. (assemble)**

_____ , each family member jumps over one of the fires and says, "I
   **4. (burn completely)**

give you my pale face, and I take your red one." The day before the New Year begins, the

family _____ a table in the main room with special foods and
        **5. (prepare for use)**

objects, such as colored eggs, cake, and the *haft-sin*, seven objects with names beginning

with the sound "s." Everyone _____ new clothes, and the family
                              **6. (cover the body with)**

_____ around the table. When the New Year begins, family members
   **7. (meet)**

hug each other and _____ gifts, especially to the children. It all
                    **8. (distribute)**

makes for a very festive environment. For the next 12 days, people visit each other, but on

the thirteenth day, it is unlucky to be inside a house, so people _____
                                                                 **9. (leave)**

and spend the day in parks and fields, where they have picnics, listen to music, and play

sports. They don't _____ home until sunset. At the end of the day,
                    **10. (return)**

everyone "_____" bad luck by throwing wheat or lentils into a river.
             **11. (discard)**

## EXERCISE 3: Phrasal Verbs and Objects

*Complete the conversations with the phrasal verbs and objects in parentheses. Place the object between the verb and the participle when possible.*

**A.**    **VIJAY:** We need about two dozen candles for Diwali.

    **NIRA:** I'll _____ pick them up _____ after work.
                             **1. (pick up / them)**

    **VIJAY:** While you're there, why don't you get some new decorations?

    **NIRA:** Let's have the children _____. You know how
                                    **2. (pick out / them)**

    excited they get about the Hindu New Year.

**B.**    **EVA:** Why do you _____ on Rosh Hashana?
                **1. (empty out / the money and everything else in your pockets)**

    **SIMON:** It's a custom for the Jewish New Year to throw what's in our pockets into moving water.

    It's like getting rid of last year's bad memories.

    **EVA:** Cigarettes are harmful. Here's my lighter. Let's _____.
                                    **2. (throw away / it)**

**C.**    **MAY:** When will we _____ for the Chinese New Year?
                     **1. (set off / the firecrackers)**

    **NING:** Not until dark.

    **MAY:** Don't the firecrackers have something to do with evil spirits?

    **NING:** Yes. We believe that the noise _____.
                                  **2. (keep away / them)**

**D.**    **LIAM:** Are you decorating for Christmas?

    **ZOÉ:** No, we're _____ for Kwanzaa, the
                    **1. (hang up / these streamers)**

    African-American harvest celebration. It comes at the same time as Christmas and

    New Year's Day.

    **LIAM:** What is your mom putting on the table?

    **ZOÉ:** A *kinara*. We _____ to hold the Kwanzaa candles.
                              **2. (set up / it)**

**E.**    **KELSEY:** Do you usually make New Year's resolutions?

    **IAN:** Yes, and I _____ because they're so easy to
              **1. (write down / all of the resolutions that I make each year)**

    forget by February.

    **KELSEY:** I need to do more than that. This year I'm going to hire a food consultant. My resolution

    is to stop eating desserts.

    **IAN:** I _____ for a few months last year. I lost more
                 **2. (gave up / them)**

    than five pounds.

## EXERCISE 4: Editing

*Read the list of New Year's resolutions. There are eleven mistakes in the use of phrasal verbs. The first mistake is already corrected. Find and correct ten more.*

<u>New Year's Resolutions</u>

Wake ~~out~~ <sup>up</sup> earlier. (No later than 7:30!)

Work out at the gym at least 3 times a week.

Lose 5 pounds. (Give over eating so many desserts.)

Be more conscious of the environment:

    —Don't throw down newspapers. Recycle them.

    —Save energy. Turn on the lights and TV when I leave

      the apartment.

Straighten up my room and make it more comfortable:

    —Hang out my clothes when I take off them.

    —Put my books back where they belong.

    —Give some of my old books and clothing that I no longer

      wear away.

    —Read about feng shui theory to increase positive energy.

Don't put off doing my math homework even when the problems

seem complex. Finish the assignments, and hand in them on time!

Read more.

Use the dictionary more. (Look over words I don't know.)

When someone calls and leaves a message, call them back

right away. Don't put off it!

Get to know my neighbors. Ask them for coffee over.

## EXERCISE 5: Personal Writing

*Write a paragraph about how people celebrate birthdays in your home country. Use some of the phrases from the box.*

> In many countries, the person who is celebrating a birthday blows out . . .
>
> In my home country, birthdays are . . .
>
> Instead of birthdays, we celebrate . . .
>
> On my birthday, I always think about . . .
>
> People in my country usually dress up / don't dress up . . .
>
> The most interesting thing about birthday celebrations in . . .
>
> We sometimes get together with . . .
>
> When we get through with . . .

# UNIT 12 Phrasal Verbs: Separable and Inseparable

## EXERCISE 1: Particles

*Complete the phrasal verbs with the correct particles.*

| Phrasal Verb | Meaning |
| --- | --- |
| 1. call _____back_____ | return a phone call |
| 2. get _____throug with_____ | recover from an illness or a bad situation |
| 3. cross _____out_____ | draw a line through |
| 4. call _____off_____ | cancel |
| 5. drop _____in_____ | visit unexpectedly |
| 6. look _____out_____ | be careful |
| 7. keep _____up with_____ | continue |
| 8. talk _____into_____ | persuade |
| 9. blow _____up_____ | explode |
| 10. turn _____down_____ | reject |
| 11. run _____into_____ | meet accidentally |
| 12. put _____back_____ | return to its original place |
| 13. work _____out_____ | solve |
| 14. go _____on_____ | continue |
| 15. find _____out_____ | discover |
| 16. turn _____down_____ | lower the volume |

## EXERCISE 2: Phrasal Verbs

*Complete the paragraphs with the appropriate form of the phrasal verbs from the boxes.*

| | | | | |
|---|---|---|---|---|
| catch on~~ | figure out | help out | team up with | turn on |
| ~~come out~~ | go off | take away | turn off | |

A. There have been a lot of changes since the first consumer

cell phones _____ *came out* _____ in the 1980s.
<br>**1.**

The original phones were big, heavy, and very expensive.

After designers _____ figure out _____ how to
<br>**2.**

make them smaller and more affordable, they really began

to _____ go off _____. Now, people all over
<br>**3.**

the world are _____ tak away _____ their mobile
<br>**4.**

phones and using them in ways that could never have

been imagined in the 1980s. Several years ago, wireless

companies _____ team up with _____ digital-photography experts to produce camera
<br>**5.**

phones, which are now popular with consumers. Internet access is another way that cell

phones _____ help _____ us _____ out _____ by keeping us
<br>**6.**

connected and informed. Today, smart phones are almost the equivalent of a small computer.

However, there is a negative side to wireless technology. For example, when cell phones

constantly _____ turn on _____ in restaurants, movie theaters, and classrooms,
<br>**7.**

they can be annoying. When we're forced to listen to other people's conversations in public

places, it _____ catch on _____ our privacy and the privacy of the person talking
<br>**8.**

on the phone. Clearly, it's sometimes best to _____ turn _____ our cell phones

_____ off _____.
<br>**9.**

*(continued on next page)*

| end up | keep up with | pick out | use up |
|--------|--------------|----------|--------|
| find out | look over | put away | watch out for |

**B.** Cell phones let us _____ *find out* _____ friends and family whenever and wherever

we want, but they can _____ *end* _____ being very expensive. It's great to stay
**2.**

in touch, but it's hard to know when to stop talking and _____ *up with* _____ our

mobile phones _____ *watch out for*. Cell phone companies advertise reasonably
**3.**

priced calling packages, but it's easy to _____ *keep up with* _____ all the minutes on a basic
**4.**

plan. Many of us have _____ *look over* _____ the hard way what it's like to pay overage
**5.**

charges. Smart consumers do comparison shopping and _____ *pick up* _____ wireless
**6.**

service with features such as free weekend and evening minutes, unlimited calls to individual

family members, and no roaming charges when customers go out of their calling area. Smart

consumers also _____ *look over* _____ their cell phone contract carefully before they
**7.**

sign it. They realize how important it is to _____ hidden fees.
**8.**

## EXERCISE 3: Phrasal Verbs and Object Pronouns

*Complete the conversations. Use phrasal verbs and pronouns.*

1. **LUIS:** I thought you were going to ask the Riveras over for dinner.

   **INES:** I did. I _____ *asked them over* _____ for Friday night.

2. **LUIS:** Did you invite their son too? He gets along well with Jimmy.

   **INES:** That's a good idea. He really does _____.

3. **INES:** If you run into Marta tomorrow, invite her too. She knows the Riveras.

   **LUIS:** I usually don't _____ on Tuesdays. If we want her to come,

   we should call.

4. **INES:** I'd like you to straighten up your room before the Riveras come over.

   **JIMMY:** No problem. I'll _____ right after school on Friday.

5. **JIMMY:** There's a big game on TV at eight o'clock on Friday that I'd like to watch. Do we really

   have to get together with the Riveras then?

   **INES:** Yes, we do. We haven't _____ since last summer. Besides, we

   canceled our dinner plans last month, and I don't want to cancel again.

6.   INES: Maybe you could pick out some CDs to play during dinner.

     JIMMY: Sure. I'll _____ right now.

7.   INES: I hope we can count on the Riveras to bring the dessert.

     LUIS: Don't worry. You can _____. If they promised to bring

     dessert, then they'll bring it.

8.   INES: You can bring out the roast now. It's done.

     LUIS: Great. I'll _____ right away so we can eat. It smells great.

9.   INES: Be careful! Don't pick up the pan without pot holders! It's hot!

     LUIS: Ow! Too late! I just _____.

10.  LUIS: I'm going to turn down the music. It's a little too loud.

     INES: Oh, don't get up. I'll _____.

11.  LUIS: Should I cover up the leftovers?

     INES: Uh-huh. Here's some aluminum foil. After you _____, you

     can put them in the refrigerator.

12.  INES: You didn't eat much at dinner tonight. You're really sticking to your diet, aren't you?

     LUIS: That's right. I've _____ for three weeks now, and I plan to

     continue until I lose 15 pounds.

13.  INES: Could you help me put away these folding chairs?

     LUIS: Why don't you rest? I'll _____.

14.  INES: Don't forget to turn on the dishwasher before you go to bed.

     LUIS: I'll _____ now. That way I won't forget.

15.  INES: We got a phone call during dinner, but I can't identify this number on the caller ID. I

     wish I could figure out who called.

     LUIS: It's late, and I'm tired. Let's go to sleep. We can _____

     tomorrow morning.

*See if you can figure out the puzzle.*

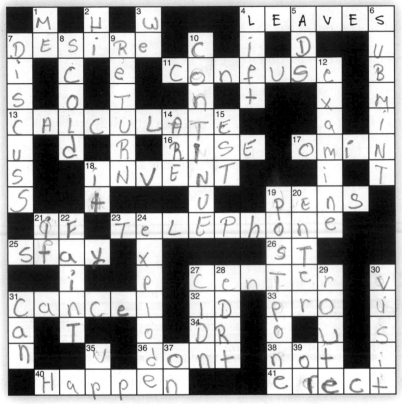

**Across**

4. Gets off (the bus)
7. Want
11. Mix up
13. Figure out
16. Opposite of *fall*
17. Leave out
18. Think up
19. These can run out of ink.
21. _____ it rains, it pours.
23. Call up
25. Don't go away. Please _____.
26. Street (*abbreviation*)
27. Middle
31. Call off
32. Indefinite article
33. Professional (*short form*)
34. Medical doctor (*abbreviation*)
36. What time _____ she usually show up?
38. Negative word
40. Take place
41. Put up (a building)

**Down**

1. Pick _____ up at 5:00. I'll be ready then.
2. Hello
3. You and I

4. Pick up
5. Advertisements (*short form*)
6. Hands in
7. Talk over
8. Tell off
9. Take back
10. Carry on
12. Look over
14. *am, is,* _____
15. Eastern Standard Time (*abbreviation*)
18. Drop _____ on
19. Put off
20. Come in
21. The music is loud. Please turn _____ down.
22. Pass out
24. Blow up
27. Her book _____ out last year.
28. Marcia always _____ up with more work than anyone else.
29. Rte. (*full word*)
30. *Drop in* means "to _____ unexpectedly."
31. You put a small bandage on it.
35. Don't guess. Look it _____.
37. Please go _____. Don't stop.
39. Either . . . _____

## EXERCISE 5: Editing

*Read the opinion piece that Luis is planning to send to his local newspaper. There are eight mistakes in the use of phrasal verbs. The first mistake is already corrected. Find and correct seven more.*

```
 ● ○ ○
```

                                                    *up*
    In my opinion, drivers should hang ~~on~~ their phones and turn off them the minute they get in

their cars. This is the best way to eliminate some of the careless accidents on the streets of our

city. After all, is it more important to keep up your friends and business associates with or save

lives and money? I have looked into this matter and found some alarming statistics on mobile

phones and accidents out. Research from the National Safety Council points out that cell phones

and texting cause 1.6 million accidents each year. Clearly, it's time for drivers to get in the phone.

And it's time for lawmakers to come over with a plan to make all phone use by motorists illegal,

including the use of headsets and other hands-free technology. They must create a law to turn into

our streets safe places for drivers and pedestrians alike. Then the local authorities must carry out it.

## EXERCISE 6: Personal Writing

*On a separate piece of paper, write a paragraph about the ways that you use a cell phone. Use some of the phrases from the box.*

| | |
|---|---|
| I really count on . . . | I'm afraid to miss out on . . . , so . . . |
| I think that I should look into . . . | Like most people, I would like to cut down on . . . |
| I usually turn my phone off when . . . | One of these days, I'm going to end up . . . |
| I'll never give up . . . | When my friends call me up, . . . |

UNIT

# 13 Adjective Clauses with Subject Relative Pronouns

## EXERCISE 1: Placement of Adjective Clauses

*Put each adjective clause directly after the noun that it describes. Draw an arrow to show the correct placement.*

1. People look at the brighter side of life.

   **that have an optimistic personality**

2. Some people assume we are born with personality traits.

   **which control all our feelings and actions**

3. Researchers contradict that idea.

   **whose work is in the field of positive psychology**

4. Positive psychologists offer practical advice for anyone.

   **who wants a better chance of being happy**

5. One activity is making a list of three good things in your life.

   **that helps to improve feelings of happiness**

6. Having a close friend also increases the possibility of happiness.

   **who cares about you**

7. Interestingly, a mother doesn't seem to be any happier than a woman with no children.

   **whose children are grown**

*Meghana is doing a research assignment about happiness. Read her notes. Circle the correct relative pronouns.*

— The dictionary defines happiness as a feeling (that)/ who comes from a
   **1.**
pleasurable or satisfying experience. A person who / whose life is happy
                                                **2.**
doesn't need to be a millionaire. The things that / who make us happy often
                                                  **3.**
have nothing to do with money or luxury.

— A woman who / whose wins the lottery might be happy, but not for long.
          **4.**
Stories who / which appear in newspapers and magazines point out how
       **5.**
quickly the money disappears and how lottery winners often end up looking

for something that / who will bring them more contentment.
              **6.**

— To achieve happiness, a job who / which is challenging or an experience
                              **7.**
that / who allows people to grow and learn is better than money. Is it the
**8.**
feeling of accomplishment that / who leads to happiness?
                          **9.**

— Research shows the importance of genetics. About 50 percent of the

differences who / which exist between a man who / whose says he is happy
           **10.**                        **11.**
and one that / which claims to be unhappy are a result of birth.

— Martin Seligman, that / who directs the Positive Psychology Center at the
                    **13.**
University of Pennsylvania, says happiness requires effort. Seligman has

clients and students who / whose feelings have changed dramatically with
                     **14.**
happiness training.

— Personal relationships are clearly important, but there's still a question

that / who bothers me. If people who / whose romantic relationships are
**15.**                          **16.**
strong feel happy, why are there so many divorces?

— Remember to look at the Journal of Personality and Social Psychology,

that / which will certainly have useful articles. Check for other information
**17.**
that / who is in the online database at the library.
**18.**

## EXERCISE 3: Subject-Verb Agreement

*Read the article about how to stay a happy couple. Complete it with a relative pronoun and the correct forms of the verbs in parentheses.*

Congratulations! You've finally found Ms. or Mr. Right. You're now a couple—two people ____who____ ____love____ each

**1. (love)**

other's company, ____laugh____ at each

**2. (laugh)**

other's jokes, and _____ to be

**3. (plan)**

together forever. Of course, you both want to make this a relationship ____that____

____Keeps____ feeling wonderful. But how? Read this advice from several couples

**4. (keep)**

____Whoes____ marriages ____Continue____ to be successful after many years.

**5. (continue)**

**Respect your partner's personality type.** Opposites attract, but they also require a lot

of understanding. Heidi, ____who____ ____is____ an extreme introvert, fell

**6. (be)**

in love with her partner Dave partly because of his warm personality, ____Which____

still always ____makes____ her feel very special. And Dave, ____who____

**7. (make)**

____respect____ Heidi's need for a lot of time time alone, gets similar respect from Heidi,

**8. (respect)**

____who____ ____Dosent mind____ his going to some social events without her.

**9. (not mind)**

**Feel lucky.** Sometimes luck is a question of attitude. Those couples ____who____

____feel____ that they are lucky to have each other are the ones ____who____

**10. (feel)**

____find____ good luck in everyday events. They don't wait to win the lottery. They

**11. (find)**

see luck in their partner's little successes and in their own happiness.

**Write your own history.** Think of your marriage as a wonderful story ____that____

____has____ a reality and history of its own. Family stories and photographs are the

**12. (have)**

tools ____that____ ____bring____ this reality back to life during the bad times.

**13. (bring)**

**Believe in each other.** Trust is even more important than love, ____that____

____increases____ and ____decrease____ during a long marriage. This is the feeling

**14. (increase)** **15. (decrease)**

____that____ ____Makes____ each partner feel safe in the relationship. It's also the

**16. (make)**

condition __that__ __helps__ people grow and change as they must.

**17. (help)**

**Spend time together.** It's not so easy in today's world, but if you want a relationship

__that__ __lasts__, it's what you need. Develop the ability to simply

**18. (last)**

enjoy being together. Couples __who__ __do__ this don't even have

**19. (do)**

to talk to feel close. Remember, your relationship, __that__ __feels__

**20. (feel)**

so perfect right now, is going to change over time. These five suggestions from successful

couples can help you appreciate the good times and survive the difficult ones.

## EXERCISE 4: Sentence Combining

*Combine the pairs of sentences. Make the second sentence in each pair an adjective clause.*
*Make any other necessary changes.*

1. I met Rebecca in 1994. Rebecca is now my wife.

   *I met Rebecca, who is now my wife, in 1994.*

2. She was visiting her favorite aunt. Her aunt's apartment was right across from mine.

   She was Visiting her favorite aunt, whoes apartment was right across from mine

3. I was immediately attracted to Rebecca because of her unique smile. The smile was full of warmth and good humor.

   I was immediately attracted to Rebecca because of her unique smile wich smile was full of warmth and good humor.

4. I could see that Rebecca had a fun-loving personality. Her interests were similar to mine.

   I could see that Rebecca who interests were similar to mine fun-loving personality

   I Could see that Rebecca had a fun-loving personality who interests were similar to mine.

5. Ballroom dancing was one of our favorite activities. Ballroom dancing was very popular in those days.

   Ballroon dancig wich was very popula in one of our favorite activities

6. We also enjoyed playing cards with some of our close friends. Our friends lived in the neighborhood.

   We also enjoyed playing cards with some of our close friends who lived in the neighborhood.

7. Our friend Mike taught us how to ski. Mike was a professional skier.

   our friend Mike who was a professional skier taught us how to ski.

8. We got married in a ski lodge. The ski lodge was in Vermont.

   we Got married in a ski lodge, that ski lodge was in was Vermont

   or
   wich

*(continued on next page)*

Adjective Clauses with Subject Relative Pronouns **75**

9. Our marriage has grown through the years. Our marriage means a lot to us both.

*Our marriage, wich means a lot to us both grown Though the years.*

10. The love and companionship have gotten stronger. The love and companionship make us very happy.

*The love and Companionship, wich gotten stonger make us very happy.*

11. Even the bad things have brought us closer together. Bad things have happened.

*even the bad things, wich hav happened, brought us closer.*

12. I really love Rebecca. Rebecca makes me feel truly happy.

*I really love Rebecca, who makes me feel truly happy.*

## EXERCISE 5: Editing

*Read Meghana's paragraph about how psychologists measure happiness. There are ten mistakes in the use of adjective clauses. The first mistake is already corrected. Find and correct nine more.*

                            focuses
Psychological research that ~~focus~~ on happiness requires a tool that can measure a person's feelings. A number of well-known researchers who they collect this type of data claim to have a simple method that works well. They ask just one question, which is "How happy are
                who
you?" People which respond to the question usually give their answer with a number. For example, on a scale of 1–10, a 1 would be "extremely unhappy" and a 10 would be
                                        who
"extremely happy." Professor Ed Diener, that is a leading U.S. psychologist, says the
                                                        who
method is surprisingly effective because it produces answers that is honest and real. Of
                        whose feelin
course there may be someone who feelings change throughout the day, so there is a related
                which
type of measurement who uses handheld computers to send messages to research participants to find out what they are doing at different times and what their mood is.
                                        who
Technology is also important for scientists which make a connection between happiness and
                                who                    has
the human body. When they see a person whose skin temperature have risen, they know the person is happy. This group of researchers believes their method of measuring happiness through body heat, blood pressure, heart rate, and brain waves is quite effective.

## EXERCISE 6: Personal Writing

*Circle the best number to show your level of happiness.*

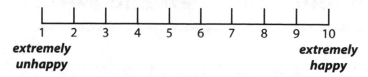

**extremely
unhappy**                                    **extremely
happy**

*Write a paragraph to explain your answer. Use some of the phrases from the box.*

| | |
|---|---|
| I am the kind of person who . . . | The thing that makes . . . |
| In my opinion, happy people are those . . . | The word that describes . . . |
| My favorite / least favorite activity, which . . . | There are people in my life whose . . . |
| The most important . . . | |

## EXERCISE 1: Relative Pronouns and *When* and *Where*: Subject and Object

*Circle the correct words to complete the book acknowledgments and dedications.*

I couldn't have written this memoir without the lessons what /(that) I learned from my parents.
**1.**

With them, I found my place in a new world, while never losing my connections to the world

that / who we left behind. The courage and creativity with which / that they faced a new life and
**2.** **3.**

culture have made it possible for me to write about our journey.

(Irina Pawlak, *Finding Your Place: A Memoir of Discovery*. Chicago, Hemerion Press, 2011.)

These stories, that / which I wrote over a period of ten years, are dedicated to my students at the
**4.**

Branton College Writing Program. The excitement whose / that they bring to the job of turning life
**5.**

into literature continues to inspire my own writing. The issues which / who we all face never
**6.**

change, but there has not been a day where / when a student hasn't taught me a new way to
**7.**

look at one of those issues. It's a debt that / whom is impossible for me to repay.
**8.**

(Patrick O'Doyle, *Fixed in Our Ways: Short Stories*. Atlanta, Sandbar Press, 2010.)

This book, which / who you are holding in your hands, would not have been possible without the help
**9.**

of many people. First of all, I'd like to thank everyone that / which I have ever met, for our lives are
**10.**

all shaped by our countless everyday encounters. Most of all, however, I want to thank the people

which / who I know best—my family and friends, without whose / whom you would not be reading
**11.** **12.**

about all the people whose / that names I never even learned. I'd also like to express gratitude to my
**13.**

office desk, when / where I spent most of the last two years writing, and to my office chair, without
**14.**

which / whose strong support I am sure I would have suffered many a backache. Finally, I need to
**15.**

thank myself for any mistakes that / where you find in these pages. They are mine and mine alone.
**16.**

(Wolfgang Fremder, *Strangers and Other Friends*, Los Angeles, Knollcrest Books, 2008.)

I'd like to dedicate this book to Jean Auel, <u>which / whose</u> novel *The Clan of the Cave Bear* I read as
                                                    **17.**

a twelve-year-old. Lost in her story, I knew immediately that I wanted to study archeology. I hope

the young adults for <u>whom / who</u> I wrote this book will find the subject as fascinating as I did.
                          **18.**

Among all the people <u>that / where</u> I must thank, first is photographer Eli Garcia-Ramirez, on
                            **19.**

<u>whom / whose</u> photographs I based my earliest studies. At Altamira, <u>that / where</u> I first saw cave
   **20.**                                                                        **21.**

paintings up close, I met other researchers in <u>whose / who</u> warm welcome I found the courage to
                                                     **22.**

keep on working. In 2009, <u>where / when</u> the book was as good as I could make it, my luck
                               **23.**

continued in my editor Jack Poulson, from <u>which / whom</u> I learned how to make it even better.
                                                **24.**

(Melissa Cho, *Rock On! Stone Age Cave Paintings in Altamira*. Toronto, Breadlow Press, 2010.)

## EXERCISE 2: Adjective Clauses with Relative Pronouns or *When* and *Where*

*Read the article about book dedications and acknowledgments. Complete the information with* **who(m)**, **which**, **that**, **whose**, **when**, *or* **where**, *and the correct forms of the verbs in parentheses.*

To L. F., without _____ <u>whose</u> _____ encouragement . . .
                              **1.**

Dedication and acknowledgement pages are the places _____ an author
                                                              **2.**

_____ the people _____ support and assistance he or she
   **3. (thank)**                    **4.**

_____ valuable while writing. These words of gratitude are an issue because
   **5. (find)**

they are probably the last ones _____ the author _____
                                         **6.**                          **7. (write)**

for a book, but they'll most likely be the first ones _____ other people
                                                              **8.**

_____ . This fact may explain some of the problems _____
   **9. (read)**                                                        **10.**

writers _____ when preparing these pages. The thanks should be gracious
          **11. (face)**

and well written, but the task of writing them most often comes at the end of a long

project—a time _____ an author sometimes _____ words.
                    **12.**                                  **13. (run out of)**

In the 16th and 17th centuries, _____ rich nobles _____
                                         **14.**                          **15. (support)**

artists, writers were often paid well for writing dedications in _____ they
                                                                      **16.**

_____ their wealthy employers. Some "authors" avoided poverty by making
   **17. (praise)**

a profession of dedication writing. They traveled the countryside carrying fake books into

(*continued on next page*)

_____ they _____ a new dedication: when each rich
  18.                    19. (insert)
family invited them to stay at their home.

   The current generation of writers usually dedicates a book to a family member, friend, or

colleague with _____ he or she _____ deeply connected.
                        20.                           21. (feel)
The dedication page is short and often contains only the initials of the person or persons to

_____ the author _____ the work. However, in the
       22.                          23. (dedicate)
acknowledgements, _____ the author _____ more room,
                              24.                         25. (have)
everyone from reference librarians to proofreaders is thanked.

   Unfortunately, most writers' handbooks give authors very little help with dedications and

acknowledgments. "It's just something _____ you _____
                                              26.                      27. (be supposed to)
know how to handle," complains one author.


## EXERCISE 3: Adjective Clauses with Relative Pronouns or *When* and *Where*

*Combine the pairs of sentences, using* **who(m), which, that, whose, when,** *or* **where.** *Make
the second sentence in each pair an adjective clause. Make any other necessary changes.*

1. Jean M. Auel wrote a novel. I enjoyed reading it.

   *Jean M. Auel wrote a novel which I enjoyed reading.*
   _____

2. *The Clan of the Cave Bear* tells the story of a clan of prehistoric people. Auel started
   researching the book in 1977.

   _____

3. It took a lot of work to learn about these prehistoric people. Auel wanted to understand the
   prehistoric people's lives.

   _____

4. The clan lived during the Ice Age. Glaciers covered large parts of the Earth then.

   _____

5. The people lived near the shores of the Black Sea. There are a lot of large caves there.

   _____

6. The clan made their home in a large cave. Bears had lived in the cave.

   _____

7. The task of hunting had great importance in the life of the Cave Bear Clan. The men were responsible for the task of hunting.

_____

8. One aspect of their lives was their technical skill. Auel describes that aspect well.

_____

9. She learned some of the arts. Prehistoric people had practiced them.

_____

10. In her preface, Auel thanks a man. She studied the art of making stone tools with him.

_____

11. She also thanks an Arctic survival expert. She met him while she was doing research.

_____

12. He taught her to make a snow cave on Mt. Hood. She spent one January night there.

_____

13. She went through a difficult time. She couldn't write then.

_____

14. A fiction writer inspired her to finish her book. She attended the writer's lecture.

_____

15. Jean Auel's novel remains popular in translations around the world. She published the novel in 1980.

_____

## EXERCISE 4: Optional Deletions of Relative Pronouns

_In five of the sentences in Exercise 3, the relative pronoun can be deleted. Rewrite the sentences below with the relative pronoun deleted._

1. _Jean M. Auel wrote a novel I enjoyed reading._ _____

2. _____

3. _____

4. _____

5. _____

*Read the student's book report. There are nine mistakes in the use of adjective clauses. The first mistake is already corrected. Find and correct eight more.*

Jorge Ramos

English 220

For my book report, I read *The Clan of the Cave Bear*, ~~that~~ *which* Jean M. Auel wrote after several years of research. In this novel about the life of prehistoric people, the main character is Ayla. She is found by a wandering clan after an earthquake kills her family. The same earthquake destroyed the cave in which this clan had lived, and they are searching for another home. The clan leader wants to leave Ayla to die. She is an Other—a human which language and culture his clan doesn't understand. However, the leader's sister Iza, Ayla soon calls Mother, adopts her.

The story takes place at a time where human beings are still evolving. Ayla is a new kind of human. Her brain, which she can use it to predict and make plans, is different from Iza's and other clan members'. Their brains are adapted to memory, not new learning, whom they fear and distrust. At first, Ayla brings luck to the clan. She accidentally wanders into a place where they find a large cave, perfect for their new home. She is educated by Iza, who's great knowledge everyone respects. The skills that Iza passes on to Ayla include healing and magic, as well as finding food, cooking, and sewing. However, Ayla's powers make it impossible for her to stay with the clan. She learns to hunt, a skill where women are forbidden to practice. Her uncle, that she loves very much, allows her to stay with the clan, but after he dies, she loses his protection. Another earthquake, for which she is blamed, destroys the clan's home, and she is forced to leave.

*Write a report about an excellent book that you've read. Use some of the phrases from the box.*

| | |
|---|---|
| One character whose personality I . . . | The main reason that . . . |
| The book which . . . | The place where . . . |
| The ending of the book, which you . . . | The time period when . . . |
| The final thing I . . . | This is a book everyone . . . |

# WORKBOOK ANSWER KEY

In this answer key, where the short or contracted form is given, the full or long form is also correct and where the full form is given, the contracted form is often also correct.

## UNIT 1 (pages 1–4)

### EXERCISE 1

2. ask, asking
3. buys, buying
4. come, comes
5. do, doing
6. eats, eating
7. employ, employs
8. fly, flies
9. forgets, forgetting
10. have, having
11. hurries, hurrying
12. lie, lies
13. opens, opening
14. rains, raining
15. reaches, reaching
16. say, saying
17. ties, tying
18. control, controls

### EXERCISE 2

**A.** 2. Are . . . taking
3. is studying
4. 's
5. remember
6. look

**B.** 1. Do . . . know
2. teaches
3. 's working
4. does . . . mean
5. don't believe

**C.** 1. do . . . spell
2. have
3. looks

**D.** 1. are . . . sitting
2. don't seem
3. 'm trying
4. doesn't like
5. writes
6. is
7. 's beginning

**E.** 1. Do . . . want
2. is studying
3. does . . . do
4. analyzes
5. write
6. sign

### EXERCISE 3

2. doesn't know
3. is focusing
4. is writing
5. looks
6. studies
7. believe
8. gives
9. are using OR use
10. convinces
11. does . . . hope OR is . . . hoping
12. look
13. tells
14. Does . . . lean
15. indicates
16. represents
17. is planning
18. doesn't leave OR didn't leave
19. doesn't avoid
20. show
21. 's
22. is investigating
23. thinks
24. takes
25. warns
26. doesn't guarantee

### EXERCISE 4

Well, I'm here at my new school, and ~~I'm liking~~ *I like* it very much. I'm ~~study~~ *studying* in the English Institute this semester, and the style of the classes is really different from our English classes in Korea. My teachers ~~doesn't~~ *don't* know how to speak Korean, and my classmates ~~are coming~~ *come* from countries all around the world, so we use English all the time. That ~~is meaning~~ *means* that I'm getting a lot of good practice these days.

Although I'm very happy, sometimes ~~I'm having~~ *I have* problems. ~~I'm not~~ *I don't* understand my classmates' names because they don't look or sound like Korean names. I always ask the same questions: "What's your name?" and "How *do* you spell it?" I want to use names with titles like "Mr. Hoffman" and "Prof. Li" for my teachers, but they want me to call them by their first names. It's difficult for me to treat my teachers so informally, but I *'m* trying. Slowly but surely, I'm getting accustomed to my life here.

I miss you a lot. ~~You~~ *You're* still my favorite English teacher.

### EXERCISE 5

*Answers will vary.*

## UNIT 2 (pages 5–9)

### EXERCISE 1

2. apply
3. was, were
4. became
5. carried
6. developed
7. eat
8. fell
9. feel
10. got
11. grew
12. lived
13. meet
14. pay
15. permitted
16. planned
17. send
18. slept

## EXERCISE 2

| | |
|---|---|
| **2.** met | **26.** became |
| **3.** asked | **27.** was dating |
| **4.** Was | **28.** didn't seem |
| **5.** did . . . notice | **29.** heard |
| **6.** Were . . . going | **30.** was whispering |
| **7.** found | **31.** got |
| **8.** didn't fall | **32.** told |
| **9.** were working | **33.** wanted |
| **10.** met | **34.** changed |
| **11.** hired | **35.** realized |
| **12.** was trying | **36.** didn't stop |
| **13.** was | **37.** broke up |
| **14.** was feeling OR felt | **38.** asked |
| **15.** was pretending OR | **39.** was moving |
| pretended | **40.** saw |
| **16.** thought | **41.** was sitting |
| **17.** wanted | **42.** was trying |
| **18.** was working | **43.** jumped |
| **19.** came | **44.** thought |
| **20.** didn't ask | **45.** didn't ask |
| **21.** solved | **46.** was helping |
| **22.** stopped | **47.** seemed |
| **23.** fell | **48.** saw |
| **24.** were taking | **49.** introduced |
| **25.** met | **50.** invited |

## EXERCISE 3

**2.** While he was drinking a glass of water, he broke the glass. OR He was drinking a glass of water when he broke the glass.

**3.** When he stood up to greet Dana, he fell on the wet floor.

**4.** He forgot Dana's name when he wanted to introduce her to a friend.

**5.** While he was eating a plate of spaghetti, he got some sauce on Dana's dress. OR He was eating a plate of spaghetti when he got some sauce on Dana's dress.

**6.** He had no money when he got the check at the end of dinner.

**7.** He was thinking only about Dana while he was driving home. OR While he was driving home, he was thinking only about Dana.

**8.** When he received a phone call from Dana, he was recovering from his car accident. OR He received a phone call from Dana while he was recovering from his car accident.

## EXERCISE 4

I'm really glad that I ~~was deciding~~ *decided* to rent this apartment. I almost ~~wasn't~~ *didn't* move here because the rent is a little high, but I'm happy to be here. All

the other apartments I researched ~~were seeming~~ *seemed* too small, and the neighborhoods just weren't as beautiful as this one. And moving wasn't as bad as I feared. My original plan was to take a week off from work, but when Hakim ~~was offering~~ *offered* to help, I didn't need so much time. What a great brother! We ~~were moving~~ *moved* everything into the apartment in two days. The man next door was really nice to us. On the second day, he even helped Hakim with some of the heavy furniture. His name is Jared. I ~~don't~~ *didn't* even unpack the kitchen stuff last weekend because I was so tired. Last night I ~~walking~~ *walked* Mitzi for only two blocks. When I came back, Jared ~~stood~~ *was standing* downstairs. I think I made him nervous because he ~~was dropping~~ *dropped* his mail when he saw me. When he recovered, we talked for a few minutes. I'd like to ask him over for coffee this weekend (in order to thank him), but everything is still in boxes. Maybe in a couple of weeks . . .

## EXERCISE 5

*Answers will vary.*

## UNIT 3 (pages 10–16)

## EXERCISE 1

| | |
|---|---|
| **2.** brought, brought | **11.** noticed, noticed |
| **3.** chose, chosen | **12.** omitted, omitted |
| **4.** delayed, delayed | **13.** owned, owned |
| **5.** felt, felt | **14.** read, read |
| **6.** found, found | **15.** replied, replied |
| **7.** finished, finished | **16.** ripped, ripped |
| **8.** got, gotten | **17.** showed, shown |
| **9.** graduated, graduated | **18.** spoke, spoken |
| **10.** hid, hidden | |

## EXERCISE 2

**2.** She graduated from college in 2005.

**3.** She's been reporting OR She's reported crime news since 2008.

**4.** Recently, she's been researching crime in schools.

**5.** She's been working on her master's degree since 2008.

**6.** Her father worked for the Broadfield Police Department for 20 years.

**7.** Simon Pohlig moved to Broadfield in 2006.

**8.** He's owned the historic Sharney's Restaurant since 2008.

9. A friend introduced Simon and Nakisha at the restaurant one night.
10. He coached basketball for the Boys and Girls Club for two years.
11. He's written two cookbooks for children.
12. He's been planning a local television show since January of this year.
13. Nakisha and Simon have been engaged for one year.

## EXERCISE 3

2. applied
3. has been working OR has worked
4. has written
5. found, was
6. has attended
7. began, received
8. went on
9. has taken
10. started
11. didn't get
12. decided
13. hasn't received
14. lived
15. has lived OR has been living
16. has recommended OR recommended
17. left
18. hasn't told
19. didn't slant
20. explained

## EXERCISE 4

My grandson and his girlfriend have ~~made~~ *been making* wedding plans for the past few months. At first I was delighted, but last week I ~~have heard~~ *heard* something that changed my feelings. It seems that our future granddaughter-in-law has ~~been deciding~~ *decided* to keep her own last name after the wedding. Her reasons: First, she doesn't want to "lose her identity." Her parents ~~have named~~ *named* her 31 years ago, and she ~~was~~ *has been* Donna Esposito since then. She sees no reason to change now. Second, she is a member of the Rockland Symphony Orchestra and she ~~performed~~ *has performed* OR *has been performing* with them for eight years. As a result, she ~~already became~~ *has already become* known professionally by her maiden name.

John, when I've ~~gotten~~ *got* married, I didn't think of keeping my maiden name. I ~~have felt~~ *felt* so proud when I became "Mrs. Smith." We named our son after my father, but our surname showed that we three were a family.

I've ~~been reading~~ *read* two articles on this topic, and I can now understand her decision to use her maiden name professionally. But I still can't understand why she wants to use it socially.

My husband and I ~~tried~~ *have tried* many times to hide our hurt feelings, but it's been getting harder. I want to tell her and my grandson what I think, but I don't want to ruin his wedding celebration.

My grandson ~~didn't say~~ *hasn't said* anything so far, so we don't know how he feels. ~~Have we been making~~ *Have we made* the right choice by keeping quiet?

A Concerned Grandmother Who ~~Hasn't Been Saying~~ *Hasn't Said* One Word Yet

## EXERCISE 5

*Answers will vary.*

## UNIT 4 (pages 17–25)

## EXERCISE 1

2. break, broken
3. cutting, cut
4. doing, done
5. entertaining, entertained
6. fight, fighting
7. forgiving, forgiven
8. lead, led
9. planning, planned
10. practicing, practiced
11. quitting, quit
12. seek, seeking
13. sink, sinking
14. stealing, stolen
15. sweeping, swept
16. swimming, swum
17. tell, told
18. withdraw, withdrawing

## EXERCISE 2

2. had heard
3. had decided
4. had won
5. had realized
6. had worked
7. had had
8. had developed
9. hadn't reached
10. had moved
11. had become
12. hadn't listened
13. had agreed
14. had been
15. had brought
16. had transformed

## EXERCISE 3

2. Had he practiced; No, he hadn't.
3. Had he met; Yes, he had.
4. Had he called; No, he hadn't.
5. Had he done; No, he hadn't.
6. Had he started; Yes, he had.
7. Had he checked; Yes, he had.

## EXERCISE 4

2. hadn't been doing
3. had been raining
4. had been eating
5. hadn't been drinking
6. had been crying
7. had been laughing
8. had been washing OR had been doing
9. had been listening
10. hadn't been paying

## EXERCISE 5

2. How long had he been living in New York when he finally received a recording contract?
3. Had he really been working as a cook in a fast-food restaurant when he got his first job as a musician?
4. Where had he been studying when he decided to enroll at the Berklee School of Music?
5. Why had he been taking courses in accounting when he began his music classes?
6. How long had he been playing piano when he realized he wanted to be a professional musician?
7. Had he been looking for ways to help young musicians for a long time when he established his new scholarship program?

## EXERCISE 6

2. had begun
3. had been studying
4. had received
5. had heard
6. had been pushing
7. had been
8. had been working
9. had been starring
10. had been recording
11. had had
12. had been waiting

## EXERCISE 7

2. After she had lost the *Star Search* competition, she signed a contract with Columbia Records.
3. She had been working at Columbia Records for several years by the time she was in an ad for L'Oréal cosmetics.
4. Beyoncé made the comedy *Austin Powers in Goldmember* after she had filmed an MTV movie.
5. When she sang in a Pepsi ad, she had already done ads for L'Oréal.
6. By the time she celebrated her 25th birthday, she had already started a clothing company with her mother.
7. She had been acting for five years when she starred in *Dream Girls*.
8. She had become internationally famous before she got married to Jay-Z.
9. When she finished the movie *Obsessed*, she had already performed at a Barack Obama presidential celebration.
10. By the time she set a record by winning six Grammy awards in one night, she had already earned millions from recording, movie, and advertising contracts.

## EXERCISE 8

My assignment for tonight was to see Lang Lang at Symphony Center. To be honest, I hadn't expected much before I ~~had gone~~ *went* to the concert. In fact, I hadn't been ~~look~~ *looking* forward to it at all. But then Lang Lang got my attention with his first two pieces.

By intermission, I had totally ~~change~~ *changed* my mind. Lang Lang ~~had played just~~ *had just played* "Hungarian Rhapsody No. 2," and the audience had gone wild. I had ~~been hearing~~ *heard* Lizst's composition many times before, but not like that. By the time he ~~finishes~~ *finished* playing, everyone in the audience had jumped to their feet and had started clapping enthusiastically. And the best part of the concert ~~had~~ *hadn't* started yet.

After intermission, Lang Lang invited several young musicians to join him on the stage. All of them had ~~been winning~~ *won* a scholarship from the Lang Lang International Music Foundation. When each child performed, I ~~had felt~~ *felt* their excitement and their passion for music. It was wonderful to see that talented children could have a chance to succeed, regardless of their ethnic background or financial situation.

Superstar quality was certainly on display tonight. As I left Symphony Center, I had to ask myself a question. Lang Lang was absolutely incredible. Why ~~I had~~ *had I* taken so long to find out about him?

## EXERCISE 9

*Answers will vary.*

## EXERCISE 1

2. I'll bring
3. Are you taking
4. He's going to miss; we won't be
5. We're attending; does the conference start
6. I'll answer
7. It's going to fall
8. We're going to see; he won't apply
9. Our plane leaves; It's going to break

## EXERCISE 2

2. will be enjoying
3. won't be harming
4. aren't going to be using
5. are going to be taking advantage of
6. will be working
7. are going to be doing
8. won't be driving
9. are going to be traveling
10. will be walking
11. is going to be blowing
12. will be drinking
13. is going to be cleaning
14. will be burning
15. will be collecting
16. will be paying
17. are going to be trying

## EXERCISE 3

2. Will the company (OR it) be paying for my wife's airfare? Yes, we will.
3. are you going to be traveling alone? No, I'm not.
4. are you going to be doing?
5. will you be stopping at the consulate office today? No, I won't.
6. Is she going to be sending the travel documents soon? Yes, she is.
7. will we be living in?
8. will we be getting to the airport?

## EXERCISE 4

2. will be talking to . . . calls the electric company
3. will be buying everything . . . does research about vertical farms
4. tries to find Toni's birthday gift . . . will be eating lunch
5. will be attending a meeting for new employees . . . visits
6. meets . . . will be taking the dog to Brigitte's house
7. will be picking up a surprise cake . . . prepares dinner
8. finishes packing . . . will be putting winter clothes

## EXERCISE 5

It's 11:00 P.M. now. ~~I go~~ *I'm going* to bed in a few minutes, but I'm afraid that I won't get much sleep tonight. I'll be tired when I ~~will~~ get up, but I can't stop thinking about my new job. Toni has our last day here completely planned. In the morning, we're going ^*to* have breakfast with friends and family. Then we're taking care of a few last-minute errands. Our plane ~~will leave~~ *leaves* at 5:00 P.M., and Toni has already made a reservation for a taxi at 2:00. I'm really excited. At this time tomorrow, Toni and I will be ~~sit~~ *sitting* on the airplane on our way to Abu Dhabi. If I know Toni, she ~~is~~ *will be* OR *is going to be* enjoying a movie while I ~~will~~ try to catch up on my sleep. Oh, no, I hear thunder. It ~~will~~ *'s going to* rain, so I'd better close all the windows. Maybe I ~~'m going to~~ *'ll* watch the rain for a while. It's a long time before I ~~see~~ *'ll be* OR *'s going to be* rain again.

## EXERCISE 6

*Answers will vary.*

## EXERCISE 1

2. will have taken
3. will have helped
4. 'll have used
5. 'll have purchased
6. 'll have wrapped
7. won't have planned
8. won't have decided
9. 'll have argued
10. 'll have accomplished
11. won't have wasted
12. 'll have finished
13. 'll have had
14. 'll have participated
15. (will have) redecorated
16. 'll have made
17. 'll have explained

## EXERCISE 2

3. **A:** How many rooms will Arnie have painted by August 5?
   **B:** He'll have painted three rooms.
4. **A:** When will Arnie have finished all the painting?
   **B:** He'll have finished the painting by August 14.
5. **A:** Will Aida have started driving the carpool by August 6?
   **B:** Yes, she will (have).
6. **A:** On August 16, will Arnie have left for his dentist appointment by 4:00?
   **B:** Yes, he will (have).
7. **A:** Will Aida have unpacked all the fall clothing by August 23?
   **B:** No, she won't (have).

8. **A:** How many quarts of blueberries will Corrie have picked by August 19?

   **B:** She'll have picked three quarts of blueberries.

9. **A:** How many pies will Aida have baked by August 21?

   **B:** She'll have baked six pies.

10. **A:** Will they have finished packing for the trip by August 31?

   **B:** Yes, they will (have).

## EXERCISE 3

2. Arnie starts the family get-together menu, Corrie and Marsha will have been picking vegetables

3. Aida will have called Arnie's sister . . . Arnie does the menu

4. Arnie will have met with the family's banker . . . Aida pays the monthly credit card bills

5. Aida finishes the fall clothes, she will have been working on them

6. the Community Center bake sale takes place . . . Corrie and Marsha won't have finished . . .

7. Arnie will have been planning his special menu . . . he goes shopping

8. the family travels to Aunt Irene's house, they will have had a very productive month

## EXERCISE 4

By your next birthday, will you _have_ made your dreams come true, or will you have ~~waste~~ _wasted_ another 12 months of your life? Will others have been ~~enjoy~~ _enjoying_ fame and fortune for years when you finally decide to take action? Don't wait any longer. The secret to your success is in our new book *Making Time for a Happy Future*. We guarantee that you ~~have~~ _will have_ found the formula for a better life by the time you ~~will~~ finish the last page of our incredible book. Without a doubt, you'll have ~~seeing~~ _seen_ the big difference that time management can make. Even better, you'll have paid only $49.95 (plus tax and shipping and handling) when you receive the key to your future. Your friends will not have received ~~yet~~ this offer _yet_. But you must act fast. Make your purchase now, or by this time next week, you _will_ have missed the opportunity of a lifetime!

## EXERCISE 5

*Answers will vary.*

UNIT 7 (pages 38–43)

## EXERCISE 1

2. doesn't it?; No, it doesn't.
3. is it?; No, it isn't.
4. haven't you?; Yes, I have.
5. does it?; Yes, it does.
6. didn't you?; Yes, I did.
7. doesn't it?; Yes, it does.
8. can I?; Yes, you can.
9. will they?; No, they won't.
10. don't you?; Yes, I do.

## EXERCISE 2

2. Didn't Greenwood build a public beach? No, it didn't.
3. Aren't there historic structures in Greenwood? Yes, there are.
4. Can't you see live theater performances in Greenwood? No, you can't.
5. Don't people in Greenwood shop at a nearby mall? Yes, they do.
6. Isn't the average rent in Greenwood under $800? Yes, it is.
7. Hasn't Greenwood been a town for more than a hundred years? Yes, it has.
8. Aren't they going to build a baseball stadium in Greenwood? Yes, they are.

## EXERCISE 3

**A.** 3. isn't it
**B.** 1. have you
   2. Didn't . . . fill out
   3. shouldn't we
**C.** 1. Isn't
   2. Didn't . . . use to be
   3. had it

**D.** 1. aren't they
   2. have you
   3. Can't . . . take

## EXERCISE 4

3. This is a good building, isn't it? OR Isn't this a good building?
4. The owner takes good care of it, doesn't he? OR Doesn't the owner take good care of it?
5. He's just finished renovations on the lobby, hasn't he? OR Hasn't he just finished renovations on the lobby?
6. He didn't paint our apartment before we moved in, did he?
7. He doesn't talk very much, does he?
8. The rent won't increase next year, will it?
9. Some new people will be moving into Apartment 1B, won't they? OR Won't some new people be moving into Apartment 1B?
10. This is a really nice place to live, isn't it? OR Isn't this a really nice place to live?

## EXERCISE 5

MARIAM: You own this building, ~~didn't~~ *don't* you?

OWNER: Yes. And you've been living next door for about a year now, ~~have~~ *haven't* you?

MARIAM: That's right. But I'm interested in moving. There's a vacant apartment in your building, isn't ~~it~~ *there*?

OWNER: Yes. It's a one-bedroom on the fourth floor. The rent is $900 a month, plus utilities.

MARIAM: Wow! That's a lot of money, isn't it? ~~Could you not~~ *Couldn't you* lower the rent a little?

OWNER: Wait a minute! You came over here to talk to me, ~~haven't~~ *didn't* you? You want to live here, don't you?

MARIAM: ~~No~~ *Yes*. I love this building. It would be perfect for me, but I can't pay $900 a month.

OWNER: But this is an historic structure. I was originally planning to charge $1,000 a month.

MARIAM: I know. The history is what attracted me in the first place. But the elevator isn't working, ~~isn't~~ *is* it?

OWNER: No, it isn't. OK, so if I lower the rent, you'll do some things in the apartment like painting, won't ~~they~~ *you*?

MARIAM: Definitely. And I'm going to pay $700 a month, ~~amn't~~ *aren't* I?

OWNER: OK, OK. And you can move in next weekend, ~~can~~ *can't* you?

MARIAM: It's a deal!

## EXERCISE 6

*Answers will vary.*

---

### UNIT 8 (pages 44–48)

## EXERCISE 1

2. isn't
3. hasn't
4. so
5. Neither
6. won't
7. and
8. either
9. did Olga
10. too

## EXERCISE 2

A. 2. didn't either
3. am too
4. did too
5. so did
6. but . . . don't

B. 1. but . . . didn't
2. neither had
3. so did
4. but . . . wasn't

C. 1. are too
2. so will

## EXERCISE 3

2. but Pleucadeuc wasn't
3. and neither does Beijing OR and Beijing doesn't either
4. but the Pleucadeuc and Beijing festivals are
5. and Pleucadeuc will too OR and so will Pleucadeuc
6. and so should participants at Pleucadeuc OR and participants at Pleucadeuc should too
7. and the Beijing festival doesn't either OR and neither does the Beijing festival
8. and so does Pleucadeuc OR and Pleucadeuc does too
9. but triplets, quads, and quints don't
10. and neither did Beijing OR and Beijing didn't either
11. and their families have too OR and so have their families

## EXERCISE 4

Twinsburg really knows how to throw a party! I went to the festival in 2010. My twin sister and my cousins ~~do~~ *did* too. We had a great time. I really enjoyed the line dancing, and so did my sister. I had never done that kind of dancing before, but once I started, I couldn't stop, and neither ~~can~~ *could* she. To be honest, I was hoping to see a cute guy twin at the dance, and my sister ~~did~~ *was* too, but we were out of luck. I didn't meet anyone, and my sister didn't ~~neither~~ *either*. But we still had fun. Our favorite part was the picnic on Friday night. I loved seeing all the other twins there, and ~~did my sister too~~ *my sister did too* OR *so did my sister*.

I have always liked being a twin, but my sister ~~has~~ *hasn't*. The Twinsburg festival changed all that. By Saturday morning, she was really excited. Of course I was too. We couldn't wait for the Double-Take Parade to start. My sister and I both marched in the parade. I felt really proud and excited to be a part of it. ~~So she did~~ *And so did she* OR *And she did too*.

Attending the Twins Day Festival with my sister may be a factor in why I liked it so much, but my cousins aren't twins, and they can't wait to go back. My sister and I think the festival is fantastic, and they ~~are~~ *do* too.

## EXERCISE 5

*Answers will vary.*

## EXERCISE 1

| | |
|---|---|
| 3. to watch | 12. watching |
| 4. to watch | 13. watching |
| 5. to watch | 14. watching |
| 6. to watch OR watching | 15. to watch |
| 7. to watch | 16. watching |
| 8. watching | 17. watching |
| 9. to watch | 18. watching |
| 10. watching | 19. to watch |
| 11. to watch OR watching | 20. to watch |

## EXERCISE 2

| | |
|---|---|
| 2. watching | 18. not permitting |
| 3. to recall | 19. to watch |
| 4. hearing | 20. to understand |
| 5. to calm | 21. making |
| 6. Sponsoring | 22. to develop |
| 7. to limit | 23. (to) get rid of |
| 8. to participate | 24. to offer |
| 9. creating | 25. to advertise |
| 10. to preview | 26. to decrease |
| 11. having | 27. not to continue |
| 12. to believe | 28. to avoid OR avoiding |
| 13. viewing | 29. not to pay |
| 14. interacting | 30. to investigate |
| 15. to behave | 31. to schedule |
| 16. to produce | 32. turning on |
| 17. limiting OR to limit | |

## EXERCISE 3

2. unwilling OR not willing to change
3. used to putting
4. fed up with seeing
5. likely to hit
6. force . . . to rate
7. hesitate to tell
8. decided to run
9. stopped showing
10. dislike turning off
11. insist on changing
12. forbid . . . to turn on
13. permit . . . to tune in
14. consider using
15. advise . . . to do
16. keep communicating
17. hesitate to ask
18. agreeing to speak

## EXERCISE 4

2. A V-chip interferes with Annie's (OR Annie) watching violent shows.
3. The show encourages them to get interested in books.
4. Her father told Jennifer not to watch cop shows anymore.
5. The teacher recommended their watching news for children.
6. Bob didn't (OR doesn't) remember their (OR them) seeing that game.
7. Sharif's parents persuaded him not to watch the cartoon.
8. The mother insisted on Sara's (OR Sara) turning off the TV.
9. Aziza wanted (OR wants) Ben to change the channel.
10. Nick can't get used to Paul's (OR Paul) watching a Spanish-language news program.

## EXERCISE 5

I'm tired of ~~hear~~ *hearing* that violence on TV causes violence at home, in school, and on the streets. Almost all young people watch TV, but not all of them are involved in committing crimes! In fact, very few people choose ~~acting~~ *to act* in violent ways. ~~To watch~~ *Watching* TV, therefore, is not the cause.

Groups like the American Medical Society should stop making a point of ~~to tell~~ *telling* people what to watch. If we want ~~living~~ *to live* in a free society, it is necessary ~~having~~ *to have* freedom of choice. Children need ~~learn~~ *to learn* values from their parents. It should be the parents' responsibility alone ~~deciding~~ *to decide* what their child can or cannot watch. The government and other interest groups should avoid ~~to interfere~~ *interfering* in these personal decisions. Limiting our freedom of choice is not the answer. If parents teach their children ~~respecting~~ *to respect* life, children can enjoy ~~to watch~~ *watching* TV without any negative effects.

## EXERCISE 6

*Answers will vary.*

## UNIT 10 (pages 56–60)

### EXERCISE 1

| | | |
|---|---|---|
| 2. let | 7. get | 12. help |
| 3. help | 8. help | 13. have |
| 4. makes | 9. gets | 14. make |
| 5. make | 10. let | |
| 6. get | 11. makes | |

### EXERCISE 2

| | |
|---|---|
| 2. you keep | 9. her play |
| 3. you (to) decide | 10. him (to) adjust |
| 4. them give | 11. him spend |
| 5. her to do | 12. him to obey |
| 6. them take care of | 13. him understand |
| 7. them to realize | 14. you (to) relax |
| 8. him to calm down | 15. us provide |

### EXERCISE 3

2. got him to agree to adopt a dog or a cat.
3. let him make the choice.
4. made him do some research on pet care.
5. didn't help him do the research. OR didn't help him to do the research.
6. got her to fill out and sign the adoption application forms.
7. had him explain the adoption process (to her).
8. didn't make him pay the adoption fees.

### EXERCISE 4

Thanks for staying in touch. Your emails always
make me ~~to~~ smile—even when I'm feeling stressed.
Knowing that I have a good friend like you really
helps me ~~relaxing~~ relax and not take things so seriously.

At the end of last semester, my roommates and I
decided to get a dog. Actually, my roommates made
the decision and then got me to go along with it. I
made them promise to take care of the dog, but
guess who's doing most of the work?! Don't
misunderstand me. I love Ellie and appreciate what
a great companion she is. I take her for a walk every
morning and every night and ~~make~~ let her run and play
in the park near our apartment as often as I can
because I know how much she enjoys it. Still, I wish
I could have my roommates ~~to~~ spend just an hour a
week with "our" dog. At this point, I can't even get
them ~~feeding~~ to feed Ellie, and now they want to move to an

apartment complex that won't let us ~~to have~~ have a dog.
I think I'm going to have to choose whether to live
with my roommates or with Ellie—and I think I'm
going to choose Ellie!

### EXERCISE 5

*Answers will vary.*

## UNIT 11 (pages 61–65)

### EXERCISE 1

| | | |
|---|---|---|
| 2. up | 7. over | 12. down |
| 3. over | 8. out | 13. up |
| 4. ahead | 9. back | 14. down |
| 5. out | 10. out | 15. off |
| 6. down | 11. up | 16. up |

### EXERCISE 2

| | |
|---|---|
| 2. cut down | 7. gets together |
| 3. put together | 8. give out |
| 4. burns up | 9. go out |
| 5. sets up | 10. go back |
| 6. puts on | 11. throws away |

### EXERCISE 3

A. 2. pick them out
B. 1. empty out the money and everything else in your pockets
   2. throw it away
C. 1. set the firecrackers off
   2. keeps them away
D. 1. hanging these streamers up
   2. set it up
E. 1. write down all of the resolutions that I make each year
   2. gave them up

### EXERCISE 4

Wake ~~out~~ up earlier. (No later than 7:30!)
Work out at the gym at least 3 times a week.

Lose 5 pounds. (Give ~~over~~ up eating so many desserts.)

Be more conscious of the environment:
—Don't throw ~~down~~ away OR out newspapers. Recycle them.
—Save energy. Turn ~~on~~ off OR out the lights and TV when I
leave the apartment.

Straighten up my room and make it more
comfortable:

—Hang ~~out~~ *up* my clothes when I take ~~off them~~ *them off*.

—Put my books back where they belong.

—Give some of my old books and clothing that I no longer wear ~~away~~ *away*.

—Read about feng shui theory to increase positive energy.

Don't put off doing my math homework even when the problems seem complex. Finish the assignments, and hand ~~in them~~ *them in* on time!

Read more.

Use the dictionary more. (Look ~~over~~ *up* words I don't know.)

When someone calls and leaves a message, call them back right away. Don't put ~~off it~~ *it off*!

Get to know my neighbors. Ask them for coffee ~~over~~ *over*.

## EXERCISE 5

*Answers will vary.*

## UNIT 12 (pages 66–71)

## EXERCISE 1

2. over
3. out
4. off
5. in (on) OR by
6. out
7. on OR up
8. into
9. up
10. down
11. into
12. back
13. out
14. on
15. out
16. down

## EXERCISE 2

A.
2. figured out
3. catch on
4. turning on
5. teamed up with
6. help . . . out
7. go off
8. takes away
9. turn . . . off

B.
1. keep up with
2. end up
3. put . . . away
4. use up
5. found out
6. pick out
7. look over
8. watch out for

## EXERCISE 3

2. get along (well) with him
3. run into her
4. straighten it up
5. gotten together with them
6. pick them out OR pick some out
7. count on them
8. bring it out
9. picked it up
10. turn it down
11. cover them up
12. stuck to it
13. put them away
14. turn it on
15. figure it out

## EXERCISE 4

## EXERCISE 5

In my opinion, drivers should hang ~~on~~ *up* their phones and turn off ~~them~~ *them* the minute they get in their cars. This is the best way to eliminate some of the careless accidents on the streets of our city. After all, is it more important to keep up ~~with~~ *with* your friends and business associates ~~with~~ or save lives and money? I have looked into this matter and found ~~out~~ *out* some alarming statistics on mobile phones and accidents ~~out~~. Research from the National Safety Council points out that cell phones and texting cause 1.6 million accidents each year. Clearly, it's time for drivers to get ~~in~~ *off* the phone. And it's time for lawmakers to come ~~over~~ *up* with a plan to make all phone use by motorists illegal, including the use of headsets and other hands-free technology. They must create a law to turn into ~~our streets~~ *our streets* safe places for drivers and pedestrians alike. Then the local authorities must carry out ~~it~~ *it*.

## EXERCISE 6

*Answers will vary.*

## UNIT 13 (pages 72–77)

## EXERCISE 1

2. Some people assume we are born with personality traits which control all our feelings and actions.
3. Researchers whose work is in the field of positive psychology contradict that idea.
4. Positive psychologists offer practical advice for anyone who wants a better chance of being happy.
5. One activity that helps to improve feelings of happiness is making a list of three good things in your life.
6. Having a close friend who cares about you also increases the possibility of happiness.
7. Interestingly, a mother whose children are grown doesn't seem to be any happier than a woman with no children.

## EXERCISE 2

| | | |
|---|---|---|
| 2. whose | 8. that | 14. whose |
| 3. that | 9. that | 15. that |
| 4. who | 10. which | 16. whose |
| 5. which | 11. who | 17. which |
| 6. that | 12. that | 18. that |
| 7. which | 13. who | |

## EXERCISE 3

| | |
|---|---|
| 2. laugh | 12. that has |
| 3. plan | 13. that OR which bring |
| 4. that keeps | 14. which increases |
| 5. whose . . . continue | 15. decreases |
| 6. who is | 16. that OR which makes |
| 7. which . . . makes | 17. that helps |
| 8. who respects | 18. that OR which lasts |
| 9. who doesn't mind | 19. who do |
| 10. that OR who feel | 20. which feels |
| 11. who OR that find | |

## EXERCISE 4

2. She was visiting her favorite aunt, whose apartment was right across from mine.
3. I was immediately attracted to Rebecca because of her unique smile, which was full of warmth and good humor.
4. I could see that Rebecca, whose interests were similar to mine, had a fun-loving personality.
5. Ballroom dancing, which was very popular in those days, was one of our favorite activities.
6. We also enjoyed playing cards with some of our close friends who (OR that) lived in the neighborhood.
7. Our friend Mike, who was a professional skier, taught us how to ski.
8. We got married in a ski lodge that (OR which) was in Vermont.
9. Our marriage, which means a lot to us both, has grown through the years.
10. The love and companionship that (OR which) make us very happy have gotten stronger.
11. Even the bad things that (OR which) have happened have brought us closer together.
12. I really love Rebecca, who makes me feel truly happy.

## EXERCISE 5

Psychological research that ~~focus~~ *focuses* on happiness requires a tool that can measure a person's feelings. A number of well-known researchers who ~~they~~ collect this type of data claim to have a simple method that ~~work~~ *works* well. They ask just one question, which is "How happy are you?" People ~~which~~ *who OR that* respond to the question usually give their answer with a number. For example, on a scale of 1–10, a 1 would be "extremely unhappy" and a 10 would be "extremely happy." Professor Ed Diener, ~~that~~ *who* is a leading U.S. psychologist, says the method is surprisingly effective because it produces answers that ~~is~~ *are* honest and real. Of course there may be someone ~~who~~ *whose* feelings change throughout the day, so there is a related type of measurement ~~who~~ *that OR which* uses handheld computers to send messages to research participants to find out what they are doing at different times and what their mood is. Technology is also important for scientists ~~which~~ *who OR that* make a connection between happiness and the human body. When they see a person whose skin temperature ~~have~~ *has* risen, they know the person is happy. This group of researchers believes their method of measuring happiness through body heat, blood pressure, heart rate, and brain waves is quite effective.

## EXERCISE 6

*Answers will vary.*

## UNIT 14 (pages 78–83)

## EXERCISE 1

| | | |
|---|---|---|
| 2. that | 10. that | 18. whom |
| 3. which | 11. who | 19. that |
| 4. which | 12. whom | 20. whose |
| 5. that | 13. whose | 21. where |
| 6. which | 14. where | 22. whose |
| 7. when | 15. whose | 23. when |
| 8. that | 16. that | 24. whom |
| 9. which | 17. whose | |

## EXERCISE 2

| | |
|---|---|
| 2. where | 15. supported |
| 3. thanks | 16. which |
| 4. whose | 17. praised |
| 5. finds, has found, OR found | 18. which |
| | 19. inserted |
| 6. which OR that | 20. whom |
| 7. writes | 21. feels |
| 8. which OR that | 22. whom |
| 9. read | 23. dedicates OR has dedicated |
| 10. which OR that | |
| 11. face | 24. where |
| 12. when | 25. has |
| 13. runs out of OR has run out of | 26. which OR that |
| | 27. are supposed to |
| 14. when | |

## EXERCISE 3

2. *The Clan of the Cave Bear*, which Auel started researching in 1977, tells the story of a clan of prehistoric people.
3. It took a lot of work to learn about these prehistoric people, whose lives Auel wanted to understand.
4. The clan lived during the Ice Age, when glaciers covered large parts of the Earth.
5. The people lived near the shores of the Black Sea, where there are a lot of large caves.
6. The clan made their home in a large cave where bears had lived.
7. The task of hunting, which the men were responsible for, had great importance in the life of the Cave Bear Clan. OR The task of hunting, for which the men were responsible, had great importance in the life of the Cave Bear Clan.

8. One aspect of their lives which (OR that) Auel describes well was their technical skill.
9. She learned some of the arts that (OR which) prehistoric people had practiced.
10. In her preface, Auel thanks a man with whom she studied the art of making stone tools. OR Auel thanks a man who (OR whom) (OR that) she studied the art of making stone tools with.
11. She also thanks an Arctic survival expert who (OR whom) (OR that) she met while she was doing research.
12. He taught her to make a snow cave on Mt. Hood, where she spent one January night.
13. She went through a difficult time when she couldn't write.
14. A fiction writer whose lecture she attended inspired her to finish her book.
15. Jean Auel's novel, which she published in 1980, remains popular in translations around the world.

## EXERCISE 4

**Sentence 8:** One aspect of their lives Auel describes well was their technical skill.

**Sentence 9:** She learned some of the arts prehistoric people had practiced.

**Sentence 10:** In her preface, Auel thanks a man she studied the art of making stone tools with.

**Sentence 11:** She also thanks an Arctic survival expert she met while she was doing research.

## EXERCISE 5

For my book report, I read *The Clan of the Cave*
*which*
*Bear*, ~~that~~ Jean M. Auel wrote after several years of research. In this novel about the life of prehistoric people, the main character is Ayla. She is found by a wandering clan after an earthquake kills her family. The same earthquake destroyed the cave in which this clan had lived, and they are searching for another home. The clan leader wants to leave Ayla to
*whose*
die. She is an Other—a human ~~which~~ language and culture his clan doesn't understand. However, the
*who* OR *whom*
leader's sister Iza ^ Ayla soon calls Mother, adopts her.
*when*
The story takes place at a time ~~where~~ human beings are still evolving. Ayla is a new kind of human. Her brain, which she can use ✗ to predict and make plans, is different from Iza's and other clan members'. Their brains are adapted to memory,
*which*
not new learning, ~~whom~~ they fear and distrust. At

first, Ayla brings luck to the clan. She accidentally wanders into a place where they find a large cave, perfect for their new home. She is educated by Iza,

*whose*

~~who's~~ great knowledge everyone respects. The skills that Iza passes on to Ayla include healing and magic, as well as finding food, cooking, and sewing. However, Ayla's powers make it impossible for her to

*which* OR *that* OR *(pronoun deleted)*

stay with the clan. She learns to hunt, a skill ~~where~~

*who* OR *whom*

women are forbidden to practice. Her uncle, ~~that~~ she loves very much, allows her to stay with the clan, but after he dies, she loses his protection. Another earthquake, for which she is blamed, destroys the clan's home, and she is forced to leave.

## EXERCISE 6

*Answers will vary.*